Contents

Introduction

Every day you make hundreds of decisions:

o what to eat
o whether a car is going to stop in time when the crossing lights go red
o whether to mess about in PE or actually get some exercise instead
o whether organic foods really are better for you and the environment
o how to use electricity safely
o what shampoo to use
o whether to read any more of this...

The reason why everyone in school does science is because it can help you to make better decisions about your life. Sometimes on television or in magazines or newspapers you'll see something being presented as a scientific fact when it isn't necessarily true. People often want to do this to encourage us to think like they do, or to buy their products. Knowing some science, and also knowing how to find out more about a particular subject in science, can help us to spot when this is happening and to make up our own minds.

But there's an even better reason to study science - it's really good fun and you get to find out how things work. This book aims to help your learning in science, as part of a course including lots of practical work and activities too. We hope that you enjoy it.

How to use this book

If you want to find a particular bit of science use the Contents and Index. There's also a **Glossary** (page 149) which gives you the meanings of most of the science words you'll meet in your course.

The book is divided into 12 topics:

At the start of each topic you'll find an **opener page** reminding you of what you already know about a topic, and a summary of the key ideas to come in the unit.

Then there is a set of double-page spreads on various parts of the topic, with questions for you to try and a **Language bank** of important words. The spreads are labelled **A**, **M** or **S** next to the title. **A** spreads introduce the easier ideas, **M** spreads follow on from these, and **S** spreads include some things which may make you think a bit harder

At the end of the topic there are **Checkpoints** with questions to test yourself with, so you can find out if there are any ideas you need another look at before moving on.

Cells

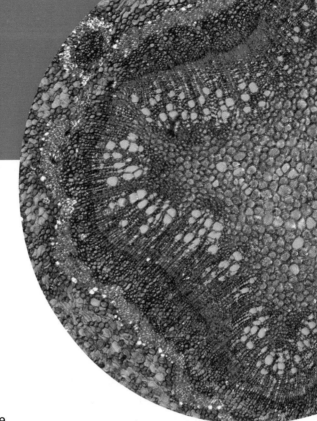

Before starting this unit, you should already be familiar with these ideas from earlier work.

- All living things carry out life processes. For example, they all grow. Can you think of three other things all living things do?
- Plants and animals are different from each other. Animals move around, but plants do not. Why do you think there is this difference between animals and plants?
- Animals have body parts which work together. You have a heart, for example. Can you name two parts of your body that work together so you can move?
- Plants also have body parts – they have roots and flowers. Name two other body parts of a plant.

You will meet these key ideas as you work through this unit. Have a quick look now, and at the end of the unit read through them slowly.

- All living things are made up of **cells**, which are the building blocks of life.
- Animal and plant cells share certain features. They all have a cell membrane, cytoplasm and a nucleus.
- Animal and plant cells are different. Only plant cells have a cell wall, chloroplasts and a large vacuole. Animals do not have a cell wall or chloroplasts and their vacuoles are smaller.
- Living things are called **organisms**. **Unicellular** organisms such as an *Amoeba* are made up of just one cell. **Multicellular** organisms such as humans and oak trees are made up of many cells working together.
- **Growth** happens because cells get bigger, and also because cells divide to form new cells.
- Multicellular organisms contain lots of different types of cell, doing different jobs. We describe these cells as **specialised**.
- Specialised cells join together to make a **tissue**.
- Different tissues work together in an **organ**.

Cells – the unit of life

O What are cells like?
O What do cells do?

Like bricks make up a house, **cells** are the **building blocks** that make up all living things. They are too small to see with just our eyes, but **microscopes** allow us to see deep inside them and examine their structure.

Cells are like tiny bags of liquid with a thin skin or membrane around them. They come in all shapes and sizes, but we know that most cells have a **nucleus**, **cytoplasm** and a **cell membrane**. Each part of a cell has its own job.

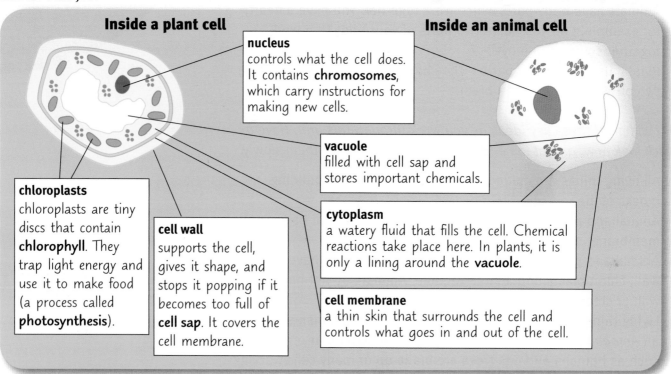

Inside a plant cell

Inside an animal cell

nucleus
controls what the cell does. It contains **chromosomes**, which carry instructions for making new cells.

vacuole
filled with cell sap and stores important chemicals.

chloroplasts
chloroplasts are tiny discs that contain **chlorophyll**. They trap light energy and use it to make food (a process called **photosynthesis**).

cell wall
supports the cell, gives it shape, and stops it popping if it becomes too full of **cell sap**. It covers the cell membrane.

cytoplasm
a watery fluid that fills the cell. Chemical reactions take place here. In plants, it is only a lining around the **vacuole**.

cell membrane
a thin skin that surrounds the cell and controls what goes in and out of the cell.

What do cells do?

Cells work together in groups to do different jobs. This ensures that the processes needed to stay alive (**life processes**) happen. One of the life processes is **respiration**, in which food is broken down and useful energy is released. Another is **nutrition**; for example, green plants have cells that use **photosynthesis** to make food using energy from sunlight.

The shape and size of cells can vary greatly, depending on the job they do. Nerve cells, for example, look and behave differently from muscle cells, because they do different jobs. We say that these cells are **specialised**, because they have special features for doing their jobs. Plant cells also show differences.

Don't confuse the nucleus of a cell with the nucleus of an atom. They are very different, despite the name being the same.

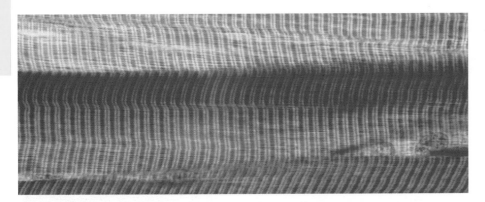

A microscope picture of leg muscle. Muscle cells can get shorter (contract), which helps them to move bones.

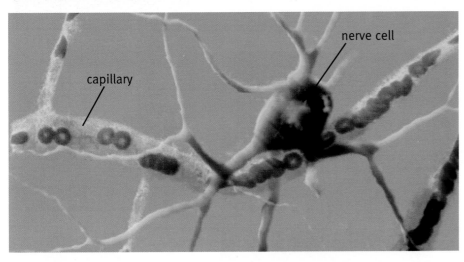

capillary

nerve cell

A microscope picture of a nerve cell. Nerve cells can be up to 2 m long. You can also see a capillary. What do you think the round cells in it are?

Constant change

Cells are **dynamic** – they're constantly changing, letting things in and out, and undergoing chemical reactions, which keep them alive.

A white blood cell (coloured blue) moves towards a yeast cell, which it will swallow up and digest. White blood cells protect the body from infection.

1 Copy and complete using words from the Language bank: Plant and animal cells are similar in a number of ways. Plant and animal cells have a _____ _____ that keeps the cell together and controls what enters and leaves the cell. The _____ controls cell activity. It is found in the watery fluid called _____.

2 Put a tick in the box if the following are present in the cell:

	plant cell	animal cell
cell wall	☐	☐
chloroplasts	☐	☐
cytoplasm	☐	☐
vacuole with cell sap	☐	☐

3 What does 'dynamic' mean? Why do we say that cells are dynamic?

Language bank

cell
cell membrane
cell sap
cell wall
chlorophyll
chloroplasts
chromosomes
cytoplasm
dynamic
life processes
nucleus (nuclei)
nutrition
photosynthesis
respiration
specialised
vacuole

Making organisms

○ What are living organisms made from?
○ How are new cells made?

Living things like plants and animals are known as **organisms**. Every organism is made up of cells.

Cells to organs

Cells are the building blocks of all living organisms.

A **tissue** is a group of similar, **specialised** cells that work together to do a specific job.

An **organ** is a group of different tissues that work together to do a specific job.

An **organ system** is a group of organs that work together to do a specific job.

Is that true of both plants and animals?

Yep.

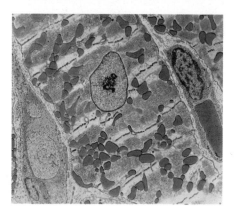

heart muscle cells
cell

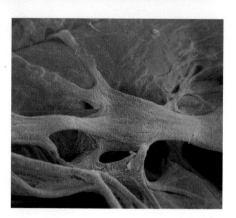

heart tissues
tissue

heart
organ

New from old

How do we grow? What happens when cells wear out or tissues get damaged? The body grows and repairs itself by **cell division**. Cells in our bodies are being replaced all the time.

Existing cells make new cells in an orderly way by:

1 **Growing** – the cell grows.

2 **Duplicating** – the chromosomes (which contain all the information about the cell) duplicate and the nucleus divides.

3 **Dividing** – the two nuclei go to opposite sides of the cell. The cytoplasm and the rest of the cell splits into two. These cells go on and on splitting. This makes more cells, so the organism grows, or repairs the damaged tissue.

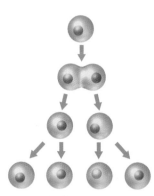

Long division: you could start off with one cell and end up with millions of copies.

CANCER CELLS

Each week, about 5,000 people in the UK are diagnosed with cancer. More than one in three of us will get cancer at some point in our lives.

Cancer starts from a single faulty cell in the body that multiplies out of control. In most cases this leads to a solid lump, or tumour. But some cancers, like leukaemia, develop in the blood or bone marrow. There are over 200 types of cancer. Sometimes cancer cells break away from the tumour and spread to other parts of the body, where they start new tumours.

The good news is that most cancers can be treated successfully if they are found early enough. Some can be treated simply with surgery, to remove the tumour. For others, radiotherapy (treatment using X-rays) or chemotherapy (treatment using drugs) may be needed to kill the cancer cells. Scientists are researching new kinds of treatment all the time. Over 800 charities raise lots of money each year to help pay for this research.

A cancer researcher.

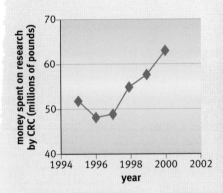

The Cancer Research Campaign is just one of many raising money to combat cancer. It is now part of an even bigger charity – Cancer Research UK, which spent over £130m in 2002.

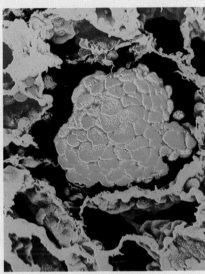

Tumour cells. The cancer cells are dividing out of control.

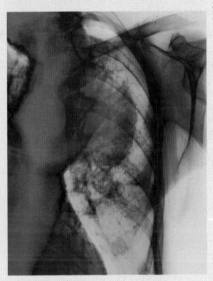

A lung showing a tumour.

---

1 Copy and complete using words from the Language bank: Living things are known as _____. These are made up of many small building blocks called _____. These join together to make _____, which work together to form an _____. Many organs work together to form an _____ _____, which does a particular set of jobs for the organism. Organisms grow and repair themselves by cell _____, which involves splitting the _____ of the cell and all the cell contents. _____ occurs when cell division gets out of control.

2 The heart forms part of which organ system?

3 Describe how new cells are made, in three stages.

4 Find out five things people can do to help reduce their chance of developing cancer.

Language bank

cancer
cells
cell division
nucleus (nuclei)
organ
organ system
organisms
specialised cells
tissues
tumour

O What do cells do?

Most living things are **multicellular**, which means they are made up of many cells. Some organisms have only one cell. They are called **unicellular** organisms.

Division of labour

In multicellular organisms, different jobs are done by different types of cell.

Specialised cells are **adapted** to do a special job and so look and behave differently from cells adapted to do other jobs. This is much more efficient than simply having one type of cell that tries to do everything. Imagine if skin cells tried to digest food...it just wouldn't work!

Some examples of specialised cells are shown below.

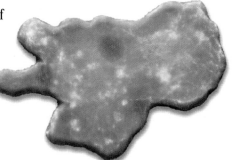

An amoeba is a unicellular organism.

	Name of specialised cell	Structure	Function	How adapted to function?	What it looks like
Animal cells	Epithelial cells	Small, fit well together. Can have hair-like structures called cilia coming from them.	Cover outer surface of the body, line cavities and protect surfaces of organs. Used in absorption and excretion of substances, or water-proofing.	The cilia provide a large surface area ideal for lining the gut, to help absorption or excretion. They may also secrete liquids to help lubricate surfaces.	cilia move — cell membrane — nucleus — mucus traps dust and germs —
	Nerve cells (neurones)	Very long, thread-like cells.	Transmit electrical signals around the body.	The long cells make up nerve fibres, which join sense organs, e.g. touch sense organs in the hand, to the brain.	dendrites — cell body — axon — joins a muscle
	Sperm cell	Looks like a microscopic tadpole. Contains genetic information from the father.	Fertilises egg, enabling information to be transferred from one generation to the next.	The tail allows it to swim about. Has a special coating on its head, used to digest its way into an egg.	nucleus — tail
	Egg cell (ovule)	Large spherical blob of 'goo'. Contains genetic information from the mother.	To be fertilised by a sperm, enabling genetic information to be transferred from one generation to the next.	The egg contains a large food store, which the fertilised egg uses to grow and develop.	cell membrane — nucleus

Name of specialised cell	Structure	Function	How adapted to function?	What it looks like
Red blood cells	Biconcave (a dip in the middle of each side – see picture).	Carry oxygen around the body.	Shape increases their surface area, which helps them absorb oxygen. Bendiness helps them to pass down thin capillary blood vessels.	
Root hair cells	Long and thin with large surface area.	Absorb water and minerals from the soil.	Long, thin structure provides a large surface area to help absorption of water and minerals. Don't contain chlorophyll as they are usually underground, so can't photosynthesise.	water and minerals enter / nucleus
Pollen cell	Small and light.	Fertilisation of the egg cell. Contains genetic information.	The pollen cell and ovule join to make a new and unique plant. This allows genetic information to be transferred from one generation to the next.	
Palisade cells	Transparent regularly shaped cells with chloroplasts.	Photosynthesis.	Sunlight passes through the cell to the chloroplasts, which contain chlorophyll. Chlorophyll changes water and carbon dioxide into food.	nucleus / cell wall / chloroplasts / vacuoles

*(Left side label spanning Root hair cells, Pollen cell, Palisade cells rows: **Plant cells**)*

1 Copy and complete using words from the Language bank: _____ cells have special functions within an organism. Their shape, form and other features are _____ to the job that they perform. In a _____ organism, there is a division of labour between cells.

2 Blood cells are easily squashed. How does this help them perform their function?

3 Root hairs are found on the surface of roots. In what way are root hairs adapted to absorbing water and minerals?

4 Find two more examples of specialised cells that could be added to the table above. Describe their structure and function, and how they are adapted to their function.

Guess what?

There are more than 200 different types of cell in the human body.

Language bank

adapted	palisade cells
egg cell (ovule)	pollen cell
epithelial cells	red blood cells
microscopic	root hair cells
multicellular organism	specialised cells
	sperm cell
nerve cells (neurones)	unicellular organism

○ **How can using a microscope give us information about structure?**

The **microscope** is an instrument we use to look at very small objects. At one time, everyone thought that small organisms were very simple things with a straightforward structure. But once the microscope had been developed, it was clear that even the smallest plants and animals were made up of units, which we now call **cells**.

Robert Hooke

Robert Hooke (born 1635; died 1703), from the Isle of Wight, was one of the greatest scientists of the seventeenth century. He invented the **compound microscope**, which was more powerful than ordinary microscopes because it had several lenses instead of just one. He became an expert in **microscopy** – using a microscope. He also improved the design of the barometer, and what he didn't know about springs wasn't worth knowing!

Hooke was the first person to draw the cells he saw under a microscope. He was also the first to use the word **cell**, because he thought that a cell looked like a small bare room or a monk's cell. This was the start of **cytology**, the science of studying cells.

Hooke largely worked alone, sometimes making notes in code to stop people from stealing his ideas, and often had arguments with other scientists. He slept little, working on problems late into the night. Despite his many inventions and theories, including some on gravity, he didn't get the recognition he deserved, and his ideas were often developed by others. He died alone, troubled and bitter.

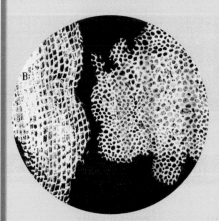

Hooke's drawing of the cork cells he saw under a microscope.

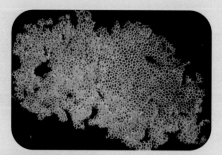

A modern-day light microscope slide of cork cells (magnification ×75). Since cells can be difficult to see, those shown have been stained with a dye to make them easier to see.

A scanning electron micrograph uses beams of electrons instead of light to magnify the cork cells. The specimen has to be coated in a thin layer of gold so that it can be seen (magnification ×540).

The microscope

The diagram on the next page shows a microscope like the one you may use in school, though yours might not be as fancy.

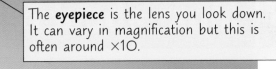

The **objective lens** is the lens nearest the object. The magnification of the microscope can be changed by rotating a different objective lens into place. Magnification is often ×10 or ×40.

The **eyepiece** is the lens you look down. It can vary in magnification but this is often around ×10.

The **stage** is where the slide with the object is placed. It contains the clips that hold the slide.

The **stem** is held in the other hand while the microscope is being carried.

The **iris** controls how much light goes through the object.

The **mirror** is concave and reflects light from the light source (lamp or daylight) up through the object. Care is needed when using daylight, so that the sun itself is not reflected through the object.

The **focusing knob** is used to move the lenses nearer to the object. Care must be taken not to push the objective lens through the slide.

The **base** makes the microscope sturdy, so it will not fall over. Put one hand under this when carrying.

The **fine focus** is used to move the objective lens nearer to the object by small amounts.

Magnification

A microscope makes an object look bigger than it actually is. We say that it **magnifies** the object. This means that the fine detail of the object's structure can be seen.

The number of times that the image seen through the microscope is bigger than the object is called the **magnification**.

To work out the total magnification of an object, we **multiply** the eyepiece magnification by the objective lens magnification.

For example, an object seen through a microscope with an eyepiece magnification of ×10 and an objective lens magnification of ×10 is **one hundred** times bigger than it really is.

1 Copy and complete using words from the Language bank: At one time, people thought that organisms were very simple, but Robert Hooke invented the compound _____ which made it possible to investigate microscopic objects. This led to the discovery that plants and animals are made up of tiny units called _____.

2 What objective lens must be used to achieve a magnification of ×400, if the eyepiece lens is ×10?

3 Explain what 'magnification' means.

4 Imagine you are Robert Hooke. Write a diary entry in which you describe a day at work.

Language bank

cells
eyepiece
focus
lens
magnification
microscope
microscopy
mirror
objective lens
stage

○ **What causes pollen tubes to grow?**

Pollen tubes and plant fertilisation
In case you've forgotten...

> **Pollination is the movement of a pollen cell from the male anther to the female stigma.**

You'll know that this can happen within a plant (**self-pollination**) or between plants (**cross-pollination**). Pollination is usually caused by insects, water or by the wind.

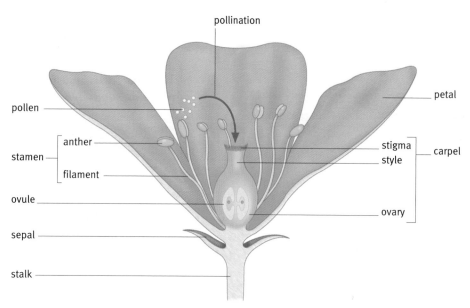

A fruit is a ripened ovary of a flower. The seeds are formed from the fertilised ovules.

Fertilisation happens after pollination. Pollen cells carry genetic information from the male part of the plant. The **egg**, which is found in the ovary, contains genetic information of the female part of the plant. The nuclei of the pollen cell and the egg cell each have only half the information contained in an ordinary cell. When they join, the new cell (**zygote**) has a full set of information.

> **Fertilisation is the process in which the pollen cell and the egg cell join together to make a new plant.**

How does the pollen nucleus reach the egg inside the ovary? For the male and female sex cells to join, a **pollen tube** must develop.

Guess what?
The role of pollen in fertilisation was first discovered by the Greek philosopher Theophrastus in 300 BC.

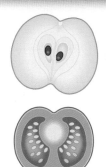

Apples, tomatoes and plums are all fruits, and contain seeds.

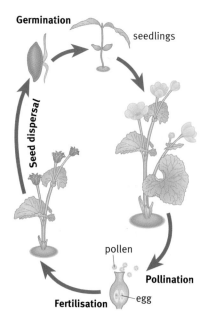

The life cycle of a flowering plant.

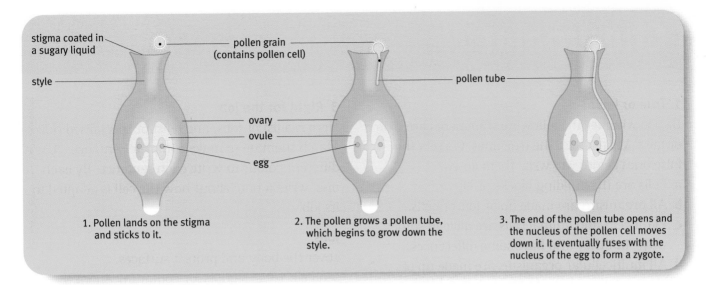

stigma coated in a sugary liquid

pollen grain (contains pollen cell)

style

pollen tube

ovary

ovule

egg

1. Pollen lands on the stigma and sticks to it.

2. The pollen grows a pollen tube, which begins to grow down the style.

3. The end of the pollen tube opens and the nucleus of the pollen cell moves down it. It eventually fuses with the nucleus of the egg to form a zygote.

The zygote rapidly divides into many cells to form an **embryo**. The ovule wall hardens to make a **seed** (for example, the pips in your apple). The life cycle of the plant then starts again.

Microscopic bad news

Look at the organism on the right. Do they look like cells? It is in fact the nasty foot and mouth virus. **Viruses** are not made of cells, but are just tiny, simple blobs of nucleus material. They take over cells and then divide and multiply very quickly, causing diseases like colds, flu and HIV. A virus is not truly alive and can reproduce only inside the cells of plants and animals.

Bacteria are cells, but they are different from plant and animal cells. The main difference is that their genetic material is not in a nucleus.

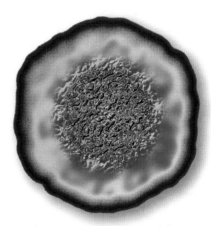

Bad news wrapped in protein: the foot and mouth virus takes over cells like a cuckoo takes over another bird's nest.

1 Copy and complete using words from the Language bank: Pollination happens when _____ cells from an anther are carried to a female _____. _____ happens when the pollen cell, which carries genetic information from the male part of the plant, and the egg cell, which carries genetic information from the female part of the plant, join to make a unique individual plant. The pollen and the egg are specialised cells.

2 Starting with the seed, describe and draw the main sequence of events in the life cycle of a flowering plant.

3 Why is it necessary for a pollen tube to develop for fertilisation to take place?

4 Find out what conditions are needed for a pollen tube to grow.

5 What is a virus? Why are many viruses harmful?

Language bank

anther
egg cell
embryo
fertilisation
ovule
pollen
pollen tube
pollination
seed
stamen
stigma
virus
zygote

Checkpoint

1 True or false?

Decide whether the following statements are true or false. Write down the true ones. Correct the false ones before you write them down.

a Cells are the building blocks of life.

b All organisms are made up of lots of cells.

c Plant cells and animal cells are alike in some ways, but they also have some differences.

d All multicellular organisms are made up of plant cells.

2 Missing labels

a Look at the diagram of an animal cell and a plant cell. Make a sketch of the diagrams. Choose the correct label from the list below for each letter A–F. Write the labels on your diagrams.

cell membrane
nucleus
vacuole
chloroplasts
cytoplasm
cell wall

Plant cell

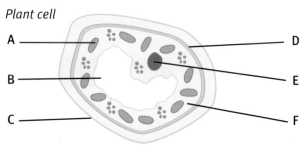

Animal cell

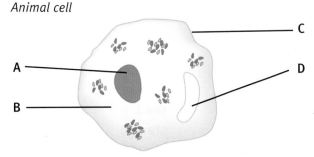

b Which labels are on both plant and animal cells?

3 Right for the job

Here is a list of jobs, and a list of specialised cells. Match them up to make complete sentences. Use a different colour to write each sentence. By each one, write a note about how the cell is adapted to its job.

Jobs

cover the body and protect surfaces.
send electrical signals for communication.
carry oxygen and carbon dioxide around the body.
photosynthesise.
absorb water and minerals from the soil.

Specialised cells

Red blood cells
Nerve cells
Palisade cells
Root hair cells
Epithelial cells

4 Fix the flow chart

The following flow chart is mixed up. Redraw it so that it is correct.

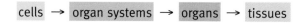

cells → organ systems → organs → tissues

5 Choose the answer

Copy and complete this sentence, choosing the correct ending from the list below.

When a male sex cell joins with a female sex cell, it is called

fertilisation
synchronisation
pollination
specialisation

Reproduction

Before starting this unit, you should already be familiar with these ideas from earlier work.

○ All living things carry out the life process of reproduction – they produce offspring. What would happen to humans if they did not reproduce?

○ As humans grow and develop we pass through stages in our life cycle. Our bodies change as we grow older. Think of four stages in the human life cycle, starting with baby.

○ Living things are all made of the same building blocks. What are these called, and what structure inside controls them?

○ Some cells have certain features that make them good at their job. What word do we use to describe cells like this?

○ Our bodies contain reproductive organs. What is an organ?

You will meet these key ideas as you work through this unit. Have a quick look now, and at the end of the unit read through them slowly.

○ **Fertilisation** happens when a male sex cell joins with a female sex cell. In animals, a sperm cell fertilises an egg cell.

○ A sperm cell is specialised for fertilising an egg cell. A sperm has a long tail for swimming and a pointed head. It has chemicals to help it digest its way into an egg.

○ An egg cell is specialised for growing into a baby. It is large and can store lots of food in the cytoplasm. It has an outer jelly layer to protect it.

○ The nucleus of the egg and the nucleus of the sperm carry information. Each egg and sperm carries slightly different information. This means that every new baby formed by fertilisation is similar to, but slightly different from, its parents and its brothers and sisters.

○ As we grow up, our organs do not all grow and develop at the same rate. It takes a while before we are ready to survive as adults. This is true for some other animals as well. Many parent organisms look after their offspring until they are fully developed.

○ How does a new life start?

New human life starts when a male **sperm** and a female **egg** join together. The creation of new organisms is called **reproduction**. Without reproduction life on Earth would die out.

Fertilisation

The sperm and the egg are individual cells, each with a nucleus. When the sperm and the egg meet, it is the nuclei of the two cells that join together (**fuse**) to form a new organism. This process is called **fertilisation**.

How the two nuclei come together varies, as all animals have different patterns of reproduction. In birds and mammals fertilisation takes place inside the female's body (**internally**). In many fish it takes place **externally**.

How you began! One sperm enters the egg and its nucleus fuses with the egg cell nucleus.

The female stickleback (bottom) lays many eggs in a nest, then the male fertilises them externally by squirting sperm over them. The male produces a lot of sperm, to improve the chances of one of them finding an egg. The male rears the young.

Hedgehogs are internally fertilised...but care is required!

Reproduction in humans

Males and females have special **reproductive organs**. The function of these organs is to ensure that the female's eggs become fertilised. The **testicles** of the male produce sperm that mixes with other liquids to make **semen**. During intercourse, semen travels down the urethra in the **penis**, and into the female's **vagina**.

From the vagina the sperm swim the long journey into the **uterus** and then up the **fallopian tubes** (oviducts). Here they meet the ripe egg, which has been released from one of the **ovaries**. If no egg is present, the sperm die after a few days.

Guess what?

Sperm are champion swimmers! Their journey from the vagina to the fallopian tubes has been compared to trying to swim the English Channel – full of treacle! Millions of sperm may start the journey, but only a few hundred will reach the egg, and just one will eventually fuse with it.

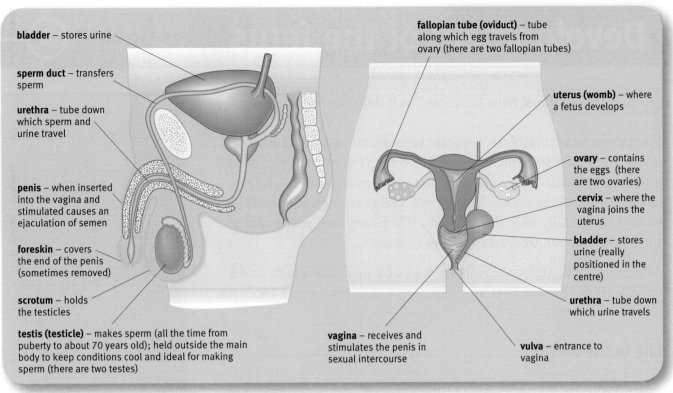

bladder – stores urine

sperm duct – transfers sperm

urethra – tube down which sperm and urine travel

penis – when inserted into the vagina and stimulated causes an ejaculation of semen

foreskin – covers the end of the penis (sometimes removed)

scrotum – holds the testicles

testis (testicle) – makes sperm (all the time from puberty to about 70 years old); held outside the main body to keep conditions cool and ideal for making sperm (there are two testes)

fallopian tube (oviduct) – tube along which egg travels from ovary (there are two fallopian tubes)

uterus (womb) – where a fetus develops

ovary – contains the eggs (there are two ovaries)

cervix – where the vagina joins the uterus

bladder – stores urine (really positioned in the centre)

urethra – tube down which urine travels

vagina – receives and stimulates the penis in sexual intercourse

vulva – entrance to vagina

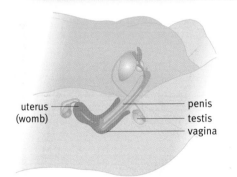

uterus (womb)
penis
testis
vagina

Humans are internally fertilised. About a teaspoon of semen is ejaculated into the female during copulation (sexual intercourse); this contains around 500 million sperm.

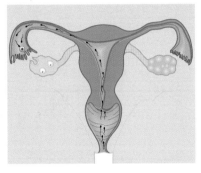

The sperm swim up the fallopian tubes to meet the egg.

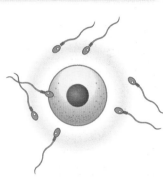

Usually only one sperm fertilises the egg.

1 Copy and complete using words from the Language bank: Animals have different patterns of _____. Some, like fish, are externally fertilised; others, like humans, undergo _____ fertilisation. Fertilisation takes place when the nuclei of the male _____ and the female _____ join together.

2 **a** Which organ produces egg cells?

  b Which organ produces sperm cells?

3 The sperm and egg cells are *specially adapted* for their functions. Explain, in your own words, what this means.

4 Describe the journey of a number of sperm from the testes to the egg in the fallopian tube. Describe where they'll go and what they'll meet.

Language bank

cervix
egg
external fertilisation
fallopian tube (oviduct)
internal fertilisation
ovary
penis
reproduction
reproductive organs
semen
sperm
testicle (testis)
vagina

O How is the human fetus supported as it develops?

Pregnancy is the time of development between fertilisation and birth. About a day after fertilisation the fertilised egg (**zygote**) begins to divide into two, then four, then eight cells, and so on, as it passes down the fallopian tube. At about four days or so it's large enough to be called an **embryo**. Eventually, after about a week, it implants itself in the wall of the **uterus** (womb), where it continues to grow.

After about nine weeks, the embryo looks a bit more like a baby and is called a **fetus**. Over the next nine months it will develop into a baby that is ready to be born.

Life in the uterus

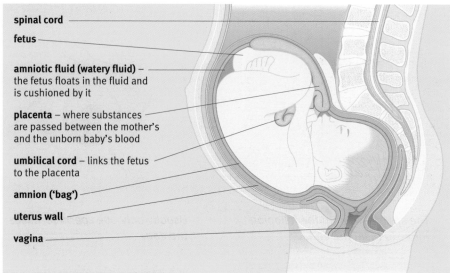

spinal cord

fetus

amniotic fluid (watery fluid) – the fetus floats in the fluid and is cushioned by it

placenta – where substances are passed between the mother's and the unborn baby's blood

umbilical cord – links the fetus to the placenta

amnion ('bag')

uterus wall

vagina

Guess what?

Some scientists believe that babies have an ear for music – even before they are born. The fetus can hear from about 20 weeks. Researchers have found that they respond to music, especially classical music, by moving about inside the uterus. The studies also showed that after birth, the babies recognised the music they had heard inside the uterus!

The zygote divides again and again.

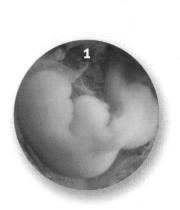

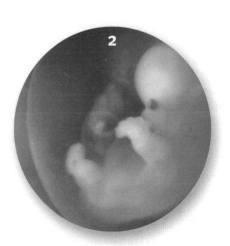

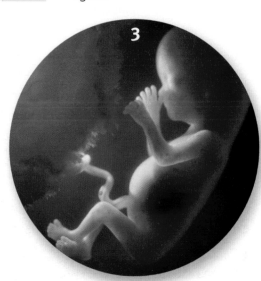

1 *A human embryo after 28 days of development.*
2 *An embryo at about seven weeks.*
3 *A fetus at about four months.*

The role of the placenta

The growing embryo needs food and oxygen to survive. A special organ called the **placenta** forms in the wall of the uterus. The placenta is connected to the embryo by the **umbilical cord**. This attaches the embryo to the mother.

Certain substances pass from one to the other:
o Food and oxygen pass from the mother's blood, through the placenta, into the embryo's blood.
o Antibodies, which protect the embryo from disease, also pass through the placenta.
o Waste materials pass from the embryo to the mother's blood, as the embryo has no way of getting rid of its own waste.

Some harmful things can also pass through the placenta to the developing baby. These include alcohol, drugs and nicotine from cigarettes. Smoking restricts the oxygen supply to the baby, and can contribute to a low birth mass. Viruses like HIV and rubella (German measles) can also cross the placenta and harm the baby.

A Canadian cigarette packet. Some countries campaign strongly to educate people about the effects of smoking in pregnancy.

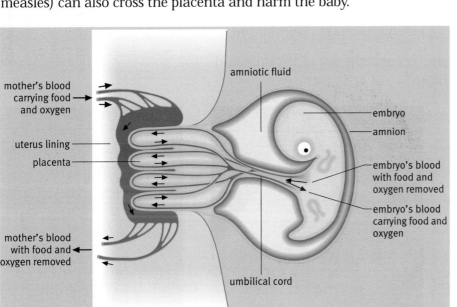
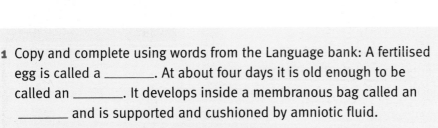

The placenta allows the mother's blood to come very close to the embryo's blood, without touching. This allows nutrients and oxygen in, and waste, like carbon dioxide, out.

1 Copy and complete using words from the Language bank: A fertilised egg is called a _____. At about four days it is old enough to be called an _____. It develops inside a membranous bag called an _____ and is supported and cushioned by amniotic fluid.

2 a What does the placenta supply to the fetus?

   b What connects the placenta to the fetus?

3 Why should women not smoke or drink alcohol when pregnant?

4 Find out what other harmful substances could cross the placenta into the fetus and affect its development.

Language bank

amnion
amniotic fluid
embryo
fetus
placenta
pregnancy
umbilical cord
uterus
zygote

O What do newborn babies need?

About nine months after fertilisation, the baby is ready to be born. In the weeks before birth, it turns to face downwards, with its head just above the cervix.

Birth

Birth begins when the muscles of the **uterus** begin rhythmic **contractions**, causing the cervix muscles to relax. This is known as **labour**. The contractions squeeze the fetus and the placenta out through the vagina. Labour can be relatively quick or can last for several hours.

As the baby comes out, the **umbilical cord** is tied and cut. The baby no longer needs this because it can now breathe using its lungs. Later, the remains of the cord will shrivel away, leaving the navel ('belly button').

Shortly after the baby arrives, the placenta and the rest of the umbilical cord emerge. This is called the **afterbirth**.

Muscles contract to push the baby out.

The amnion breaks ('waters' break).

The head moves to the entrance to the vagina.

The vagina's elastic muscles stretch around the head and body of the baby.

Birth.

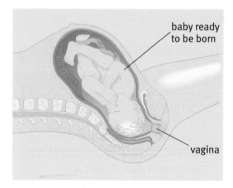

A baby in the uterus, ready for birth. The head usually comes out first.

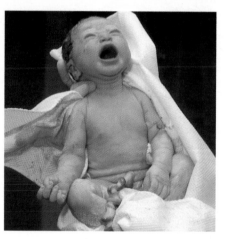

The cord is cut soon after birth.

Guess what?

Some babies are delivered by **Caesarean section**. This is a surgical operation that involves cutting through the abdomen wall and removing the baby. The procedure is named after the Roman dictator Julius Caesar, who is supposed to have been born this way in 100 BC.

After the birth

The baby is nourished by milk from the **mammary glands**, in the mother's breast. Milk provides nutrients, and **antibodies** that protect the baby from infection. Then, as its digestive system develops, the baby is **weaned** (given food as well as milk).

Gestation

The **gestation period** is the time the mother carries the young in her uterus while it grows and develops. In humans this is nine months, but other mammals have different gestation periods. Usually, larger mammals have longer gestation periods.

Different animals produce young at different stages of development. Human babies, like all mammals, develop in the safety of the uterus. But newborn humans are not developed enough to look after themselves. They're therefore completely dependent on their parents for food and protection.

The offspring of other species, like elephants and horses, are able to stand and walk very soon after birth. This ensures that they can reach their mothers' milk, and run away from predators.

A baby will naturally turn towards anything that strokes its cheek. This ensures that it finds and feeds from its mother.

Animal	Gestation period	Young
Human	9 months	Born helpless.
Polar bear	8 months	Born very light, small and helpless in the hibernation den.
Elephant	22 months	Born able to stand and walk.

A newborn elephant can walk and stand within minutes. This helps it to escape predators, but it still has to learn how to use its trunk.

Polar bears are very large mammals but carry their young for only a short period. This is because food is often in short supply, so the mother may not be able to provide her young with a continuous supply of food in the uterus. The young are born small and helpless.

Language bank

1 Copy and complete using words from the Language bank:
The _____ period is the time the mother carries her young inside her body while it develops. During labour, the muscles of the _____ contract, expelling the fetus and the placenta through the _____. Young mammals are nourished by milk from their mothers' _____ glands, which protects them from infection. Newborn humans are more dependent on their parents than the young of some other species.

2 What is the gestation period in humans?

3 Why are the placenta and umbilical cord called the afterbirth?

4 Why is it important that the young of some species are born with the ability to stand and run?

afterbirth
antibodies
birth
cervix
contractions
gestation period
labour
mammary glands
suckle
umbilical cord
uterus
vagina
wean

○ How do humans change as they grow?
○ When can human fertilisation take place?

Babies don't stay small for long. They soon develop from infants into toddlers and then into larger children. Then, before you know it, they want mobile phones and more independence! This is the beginning of the period of emotional and physical change called **adolescence**.

Adolescence

In fish all the parts of the body grow at the same rate, but in humans the body has growth spurts and certain organs develop at different times.

Puberty is the time when a child starts to mature sexually and is able to produce offspring. In boys, this usually happens between the ages of 11 and 15, while girls start puberty between the ages of 9 and 15. These changes are controlled by chemicals called **hormones**. At the same time, adolescents are becoming emotionally mature, and begin to develop adult ways of thinking and behaving.

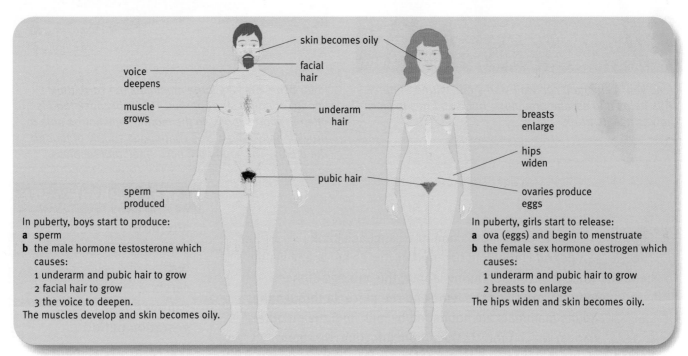

skin becomes oily
facial hair
voice deepens
muscle grows
underarm hair
breasts enlarge
hips widen
sperm produced
pubic hair
ovaries produce eggs

In puberty, boys start to produce:
a sperm
b the male hormone testosterone which causes:
  1 underarm and pubic hair to grow
  2 facial hair to grow
  3 the voice to deepen.
The muscles develop and skin becomes oily.

In puberty, girls start to release:
a ova (eggs) and begin to menstruate
b the female sex hormone oestrogen which causes:
  1 underarm and pubic hair to grow
  2 breasts to enlarge
The hips widen and skin becomes oily.

The menstrual cycle

For fertilisation to take place a ripe egg must be released from one of the female's ovaries. A girl is born with all the eggs that she will release throughout her life. But it is only after puberty, when she begins to release ripe eggs (**ovulate**), that the eggs can be fertilised.

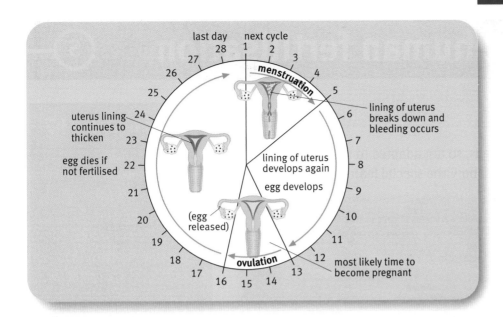

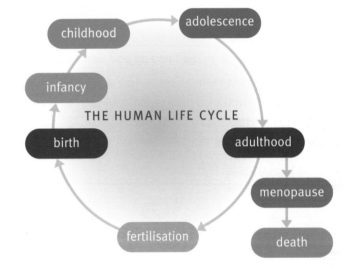

The 28-day cycle of ovulation, lining growth and menstruation is called the menstrual cycle. Hormones control each part of this cycle. The day on which the different stages begin can vary from woman to woman, and from month to month in the same woman.

In menstruation the unfertilised egg and blood from the uterus lining flow out from the vagina.

Contraception

If a couple decides to have a small family, or not to have children at all, they will need a way of making sure that sexual intercourse does not result in pregnancy. This is called **birth control** or **contraception**. There are several different contraceptives:

- the condom is a thin rubber cover that is put over the penis to trap sperm;
- the diaphragm covers the woman's cervix (the entrance to the uterus) so stops the sperm from reaching the egg;
- the contraceptive pill contains hormones that stop the woman from ovulating;
- the natural method can be used by people who think other kinds of birth control are wrong. The woman does tests to find out when ovulation is close and does not have sex near that time.

THE HUMAN LIFE CYCLE

childhood — adolescence
infancy
birth — adulthood
fertilisation — menopause — death

1 Copy and complete using words from the Language bank: _____ is the time when changes in hormone concentrations result in the development of sexual characteristics and emotional changes. The _____ cycle involves the release of egg cells from the _____ at regular intervals of about 28 days. This monthly cycle stops during _____. _____ control the stages in the cycle.

2 Put the following in the correct order: childhood, maturity, adolescence, ageing, infancy, birth, fertilisation, death.

3 Create a flowchart that shows the main stages of human life, starting with fertilisation. Label it with details of changes that occur at each stage.

4 Why do you think the menstrual cycle stops during pregnancy?

Language bank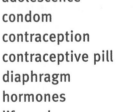

adolescence
condom
contraception
contraceptive pill
diaphragm
hormones
life cycle
menopause
menstrual cycle
menstruation
ovaries
ovulation
pregnancy
puberty

More about human fertilisation

O How does a new life start?

Sperm and eggs are **specialised** cells, so are adapted to the job of fertilisation. The diagrams below show the special features they have.

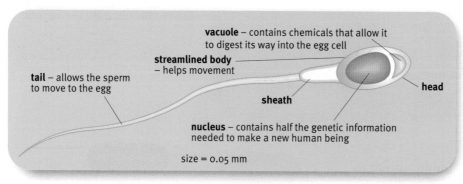

vacuole – contains chemicals that allow it to digest its way into the egg cell

streamlined body – helps movement

tail – allows the sperm to move to the egg

sheath

head

nucleus – contains half the genetic information needed to make a new human being

size = 0.05 mm

A sperm is much smaller than an egg and has less cytoplasm, as it requires less of an energy store.

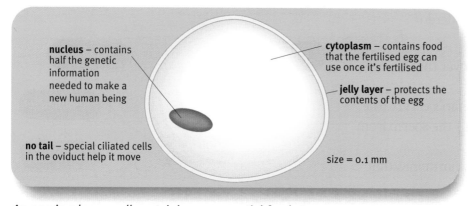

nucleus – contains half the genetic information needed to make a new human being

cytoplasm – contains food that the fertilised egg can use once it's fertilised

jelly layer – protects the contents of the egg

no tail – special ciliated cells in the oviduct help it move

size = 0.1 mm

An egg is a larger cell containing an essential food store.

Passing on information

The nucleus of nearly every cell in your body contains **chromosomes**. Chromosomes are fine threads that carry pieces of information about your **characteristics**, like your eye or hair colour. These pieces of information are called **genes**. Each of us has more than 30 000 genes. Chromosomes and genes are made of a chemical called **DNA** (**deoxyribonucleic acid**).

Most human cells contain 46 chromosomes that are arranged in pairs. The sperm and egg cells, however, contain only 23 single chromosomes. When a sperm fertilises an egg cell, a new cell (**zygote**) is formed. This cell contains 46 chromosomes – 23 from the mother and 23 from the father – all the information needed to make a new person. This is why you inherit some of your mother's characteristics and some of your father's.

The study of **inherited characteristics** is called **heredity**.

Guess what?

An Austrian monk called Gregor Mendel (1822–1884) is known as the father of inheritance. By carefully studying the pea plants that he grew, he discovered how characteristics are passed on from one generation to the next. His work laid the foundation for the study of genetics.

Sir John Sulston led UK scientists in the international human genome project, which worked out the complete sequence of all the genes on our chromosomes.

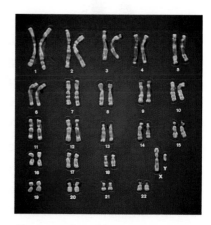

The 23 pairs of human chromosomes. Half of each pair comes from each parent.

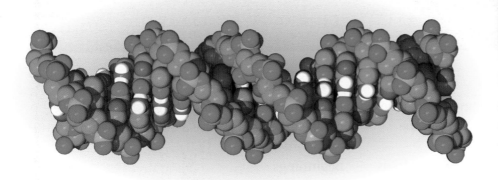

Part of a DNA molecule which carries the genetic code needed to build an organism.

Twins

No two people have the same genes – except **identical twins**, who have exactly the same set of genes. Identical twins are formed when a fertilised egg splits into two cells in the mother's uterus and each grows into a baby. **Non-identical** twins develop when a woman releases two eggs at the same time and both are fertilised.

Identical twins look alike because they have the same genes.

Non-identical twins are no more alike than any other brothers and sisters.

1 Copy and complete using words from the Language bank: Sperm and _____ are _____ cells, which means that they carry out special jobs. During fertilisation, their _____ fuse, so the offspring have a mixture of their parents' characteristics. Information about these characteristics is stored in the nuclei in fine threads called _____.

2 Explain what somebody would mean if they said, 'Paul has his father's teeth in his mother's mouth.'

3 You probably look similar to your parents but not identical. Why?

4 Find out more about Gregor Mendel. Where did he live, what did he do, what did he find out? Write a short report of your findings.

Language bank

characteristics
chromosomes
cytoplasm
DNA (deoxyribonucleic acid)
egg
genes
heredity
identical twins
inherited
Gregor Mendel
non-identical twins
nucleus
specialised cells
sperm
vacuole
zygote

Checkpoint

1 True or false?

Decide whether the following statements are true or false. Write down the true ones. Correct the false ones before you write them down.

a Fertilisation happens when a male sex cell joins with a female sex cell.

b Fertilisation happens in humans but not in fish.

c The male sex cell is the egg and the female sex cell is the sperm.

d Testicles produce sperm and ovaries produce eggs.

2 Specialised sex cells

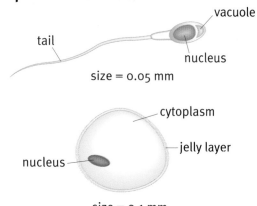

tail

vacuole

nucleus

size = 0.05 mm

cytoplasm

jelly layer

nucleus

size = 0.1 mm

Look at the diagrams of a sperm and an egg. Make a sketch of the diagrams. Choose the correct function from the list below for each structure. Write the function after each structure name on your diagram.

Functions

o contains food so the zygote can grow

o for swimming to the egg

o contains enzymes so it can digest its way into the egg

o protects the egg

o contains genetic information

o contains genetic information

3 We are all different

Match up the beginnings and endings to make complete sentences. Use a different colour to write each sentence.

Beginnings

o Sperm cells and egg cells

o At fertilisation the nuclei join together so that

o Chromosomes are made of DNA which

o The genes inside each sperm and egg

o This means that every baby is different,

Endings

o except identical twins which both come from the same zygote.

o each have a nucleus which contains 23 chromosomes.

o carries information in genes.

o the zygote has 46 chromosomes.

o are all slightly different.

4 All mixed up

Copy and complete these sentences, unscrambling the bold words.

o The **neattogis doprei** is the time when a baby is carried in its mother's uterus.

o As a baby grows up, its body changes. This is called **pelmetdenov**.

o We are not fully developed when we are born, so we are **tedendepn** on our parents to feed us and look after us.

Environment and feeding relationships

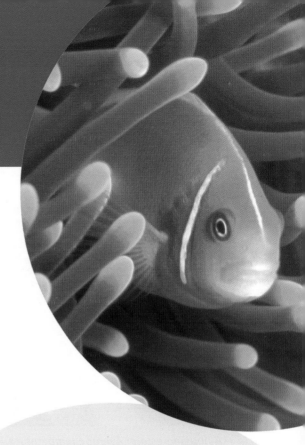

Before starting this unit, you should already be familiar with these ideas from earlier work.

- The place where an organism lives is its **habitat**. Can you think of two different habitats, and name an organism that lives in each?
- Habitats have different conditions. For example, a habitat may be hot or cold. Think of two other conditions that might vary in different habitats.
- A **food chain** shows what eats what in a habitat. For example, a squirrel eats acorns, but a fox eats the squirrel. Is an acorn a producer or a consumer? What about a squirrel and a fox?
- Some animals eat other animals. Some animals eat plants. What two words describe these different kinds of animals?

You will meet these key ideas as you work through this unit. Have a quick look now, and at the end of the unit read through them slowly.

- All organisms are different – they show variation. Different organisms are adapted to different habitats. For example, a cactus can store water and is **adapted** to living in the dry desert.
- The surroundings or **environment** can change regularly. For example, conditions in a habitat change from bright and warm during the day to dark and colder at night.
- Organisms living in the habitat are adapted to cope with these changes.
- Environmental conditions also change through the year. Some birds fly many miles (migrate) to another country to escape the winter cold.
- Different habitats provide different food, and animals are adapted to eat the food where they live. For example, parrots have strong beaks and can crack nuts, a good food source in their habitat.
- A squirrel eats beech nuts as well as acorns, and a fox eats rabbits as well as squirrels. These different food chains combine in a **food web,** which shows all the feeding relationships in the habitat linked together.

Environments

> **O How does the environment influence the animals and plants living in a habitat?**

A housing estate: Average temperature = 10 °C
Average rainfall = 90 mm per year

The Namib Desert: Average temperature = 31 °C
Average rainfall = 0.5 mm per year

These are two different places where we find living things. The places where organisms live are known as **habitats**. What is it that decides where an organism lives?

Why no kangaroos at the North Pole?

The organisms that live in a habitat are determined by the **environmental conditions** in the habitat. Environmental conditions vary from place to place, but any environment must at least provide animals with:

- O food
- O water
- O shelter

and plants with:

- O water
- O light
- O a place to grow roots

The **environmental conditions** of different habitats can vary a lot, depending on where they are in the world. Desert temperatures are very different from those in the Arctic or an ocean.

A habitat will suit some organisms better than others. We say that the organisms are **adapted** to living in their environment. A polar bear, for example, is adapted to live in a cold environment because it has special characteristics, like thick fur to keep it warm.

Examples of habitats and things that live there

Thick layers of fat under their skin — to insulate from the cold

Bodies are aerodynamic (dart-shaped) and feet are webbed — which helps movement through water

This adelie penguin lives at Halley in the Antarctic. The average temperature is −18.4 °C and 1.5 metres of snow falls each year. The sea temperature stays fairly constant at a relatively cosy 0°C.

This human is not well adapted physically to life in the Antarctic, but our ability to use tools and materials to protect ourselves from our environment means that humans are found in all conditions.

Fur — keeps camel warm through those chilly desert nights

Humps — store food for times when it's not available

Doesn't sweat much — saves water

Large feet — spreads out weight

The camel has to be able to survive long periods in the desert without water. It also has to walk on soft sand without sinking.

Air bladders — make fronds float so they can be closer to sunlight and photosynthesise. Seaweed also has sticky holdfasts for holding on to rocks.

Seaweed grows on rocky shores, which have harsh and changing living conditions. For some of the time it is in water, at sea temperatures. But at other times it's in the baking hot sun, with huge waves smashing around it.

1 Copy and complete using words from the Language bank: A _____ is place where certain plants and animals live. The number and type of organisms in a habitat are affected by environmental _____, like the temperature and how much water there is.

2 Give an example of a habitat and two organisms that live there.

3 The cactus is a desert plant with a swollen stem that stores water. Why is the cactus well adapted to life in the desert?

4 Why do you think polar bears aren't brown or black?

5 Find out two more adaptations that polar bears have to living in a cold climate.

Language bank

adaptation
adapted
aerodynamic
environment
environmental conditions
habitat

How do environments vary?

Plants and animals must be **adapted** to survive any changes in the environmental conditions of their habitat. For example, a desert may be 50 °C during the day and 0 °C at night. Other changes may depend on what time of year it is.

Daily changes

The natural rhythms of nature, like night and day, have a big influence on a habitat. Sunlight affects temperature, light intensity (brightness) and humidity. Changes in these conditions affect the organisms that live there, triggering behaviours such as birds singing and flowers opening or closing.

The animals you see in a habitat during the day will be different from those you see in the same habitat at night.

Organisms have **special features** or **adaptations** that help them to **survive** natural daily changes. For example, **nocturnal species**, which are active at night, often have good eyesight or a better developed sense of smell than **diurnal** creatures, which are active during the day. Some nocturnal animals are dark in colour, which helps them to avoid **predators**. Small bats hunt insects at night by **echolocation** (using sound to 'see'). Being **nocturnal**, they avoid overheating, attack and competition for food.

Good eyesight and almost silent flight make the owl an effective hunter, even in poor light.

Seasonal changes

In winter, the days are shorter and it's cooler. Unlike humans, plants and animals can't just put on a coat or turn up the heating. Here are three ways that they are adapted to cope with **climatic stress**.

Some animals, like the osprey, **migrate** to warmer climates for the cold winter periods and then return in the summer.

Migration improves their chances of survival as the warmer climate provides a better environment for feeding, breeding, and rearing young.

Some animals, like hedgehogs and squirrels, make **food stores** in the autumn, and spend the winter months in a deep sleep called **hibernation**. This reduces the amount of food they need, and helps them survive the cold winter temperatures.

Many insects lay eggs in places that are protected from harsh winter conditions. This is known as **over-wintering**.

During hibernation, a squirrel survives on the fat stored in its body.

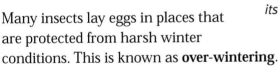

Daffodil bulbs remain dormant in the winter and grow and flower in early spring.

1 Copy and complete using words from the Language bank: Organisms are _____ to survive daily and seasonal changes in their habitat. _____ animals are active at night. Some animals _____ to warmer places for the winter. Some animals go into a deep sleep for the winter. This is called _____ .

2 Make a list of animals that are active during the day around your school. How do you think this may change at night?

3 Why do many birds eat so much that they double their normal mass just before migration?

4 Describe the adaptations of an animal to climatic stress. (Don't use one already on this page.)

Language bank

adaptations
adapted
climatic stress
diurnal
dormant
echolocation
hibernation
insulate
light intensity
migrate
nocturnal
over-wintering
predator
survival

O How do environments vary?

The osprey – what conditions does it like?

Imagine you are a scientist studying the osprey in its natural habitat. To find out more about the environment, you might:

Use a decibel meter to measure how loud the noise in the environment is.

Use a map and Global Positioning System (GPS) to find where you are, or take your measurements a known distance from a fixed point.

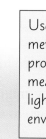

Use a light meter or light probe to measure how light changes in the environment.

Use a humidity (dampness) probe to measure humidity in the environment.

Use a barometer to measure atmospheric pressure in the environment.

Use a rain gauge to measure rainfall in the environment.

Use a thermometer or temperature probe to measure temperature in the environment.

You would also observe the bird's behaviour and record what you saw. Nest web cams could be used to help study behaviour and the nest environment.

Use an anemometer to measure wind speed in the environment.

You might summarise your findings like this:

Habitat location: Dodd Wood near Bassenthwaite, The Lake District, Cumbria

Nesting area: tall pines and artificial platform where they can shelter and breed

Food supply: pike, perch and trout in the lake

Conditions: see below

An osprey

Interpreting patterns in data

Sometimes scientists show their findings on graphs, which can help them to understand how environmental conditions affect the behaviour of organisms.

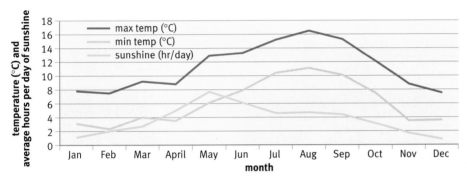

An osprey's migration route.

In mid-September temperatures begin to fall, and hours of sunshine fall more rapidly, as the days begin to shorten. This causes the birds to become increasing agitated until eventually they fly off for the African coast

Tips on monitoring an environment

o Make as many measurements as you can. The more results you obtain, the more likely your **conclusions** will be **valid** or **true**. (Though this does depend on how good your method and measurements are.)

o Always consider **the sample size** – seeing one bird once in a particular place does not mean it lives there all the time – it might be lost or off-course. Seeing hundreds might be more convincing.

o **Repeat your results** – do it again on another occasion to **double check** your observations. This should reduce or indicate an error and ensure that you obtain **reliable evidence**.

1 Why might we want to monitor conditions in an animal's habitat?

2 Why is food often in short supply during winter?

3 Why do some animals migrate in the winter?

4 Find the name of an animal that migrates to the UK in our winter. Give the main reasons why it does this.

Language bank

anemometer
barometer
conclusions
humidity
light meter
monitor
rain gauge
sample size
thermometer
valid

What is a feeding relationship?

Every living thing needs energy to stay alive. Plants use the Sun's energy to make their own food, but animals need to eat plants or other animals to get their energy. If one organism feeds on another, we say that they have a **feeding relationship**.

Blending into the background has its advantages.

The perfect predator

A **predator** is an organism that is well adapted to **finding**, **catching** and **killing** its prey – in other words, **hunting**. They generally have:

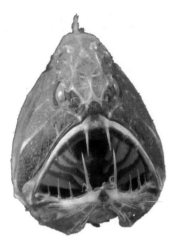

Sharp or hooked teeth, claws, talons or a beak for piercing and tearing.

Acute vision and eyes close together at the front of their head, and a good sense of smell.

The ability to ambush, trap, poison or hunt by stealth.

How to avoid it!

Prey are the organisms that are hunted by predators. They are adapted for **detecting** and **avoiding** predators – in other words, **escaping**. They generally:

Have eyes at the side of their heads for good all-round vision, acute hearing and sense of smell to detect danger, and are easily startled.

Are nocturnal, so few predators are active, and are camouflaged to blend in with the environment.

Have armour to protect them or speed to get away quickly.

Animals are adapted to their food source

Organisms are adapted to their food source. The pictures below show three birds with very different beaks.

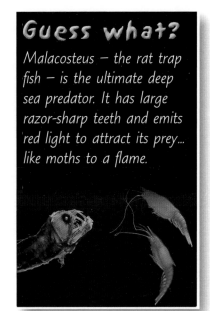

The eagle's beak is sharp, as it has to tear flesh from its prey to eat.

The flamingo's beak is long and scooped, as it has to dig with its beak to find shrimps.

The parrot's beak is rounded like a nutcracker and strong, as it has to break nuts.

1 Copy and complete using words from the Language bank: _____ are animals that eat prey. When one organism feeds on another we say that the organisms have a _____ relationship. Animals are _____ to their particular food source.

2 Draw a picture of a) an imaginary perfect predator and b) an imaginary perfect prey.

3 Give three examples of a predator and three examples of a prey, not mentioned on this page.

4 Find the correct ending to **a** and **b** using **c** or **d**:
   a The cactus has spikes on it so _____
   b The tiger has sharp teeth so _____
   c _____ it can rip flesh from its prey.
   d _____ other animals don't eat it.

Language bank ○

adapted
predators
predation
feeding relationship
hunting
prey

What do food webs tell us?

Food chains show feeding relationships. For example:

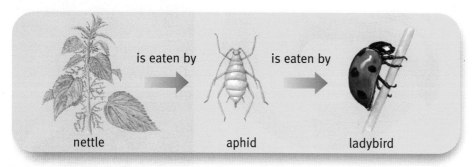

is eaten by → is eaten by →

nettle · aphid · ladybird

Food webs

Many organisms can be eaten by more than one consumer. For example, nettles are eaten by aphids as well as caterpillars. Food chains link up to form a food web, which shows all the feeding relationships in a particular habitat.

There are four simple food chains in this illustration. Can you find them?

① The nettle is a plant that makes its own food by **photosynthesis**, so it's called a **producer**.

② The grass and trees are also producers.

③ The animals in the chain are called **consumers**, because they can't make food, they have to eat, or consume, it.

④ The vole is an example of a **herbivore**, as it eats plants.

⑤ The owl is a **carnivore** (meat eater).

⑥ **Top carnivores** are found at the end of a food chain, because nothing eats them.

Humans are **omnivores**, as they can eat meat and plants.

An example of a food web.

Food chains are energy chains

Food chains are also called 'energy chains'. They show us how energy is transferred from one living thing to another.

Green plants convert the **light energy** from the Sun into **chemical energy**, which is stored in the food they make. They use this energy to live and grow. When they are eaten, energy passes to the organism that has eaten them; when that organism is eaten, energy is passed on again

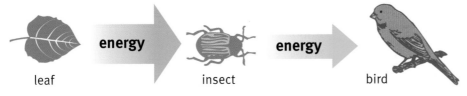

– and so on, along the food chain.

Population and community

A group of any one species of organism in a habitat is known as the **population** of that species. A **community** is all the populations of all species living together in the same area.

1 Copy and complete using words from the Language bank: All the organisms in a habitat can be linked together in food _____. Food _____ are made up of a number of food chains, which always start with plants. _____ is passed from one organism in the food chain to the next, but some is lost at each step.

2 Draw up a food chain in which humans are the consumers.

3 'Organisms in a habitat compete for resources from the environment.' Explain what you think this means your own words.

Owl faeces. Not all the energy in the prey passes to the predator. The bones of this rodent couldn't be digested, so simply passed through the owl in its faeces. So a bird has to eat many rodents to stay alive.

Language bank

- carnivore
- community
- consumer
- energy
- feeding relationship
- food chains
- food webs
- herbivore
- omnivore
- photosynthesis
- population
- producer
- top carnivore

Checkpoint

1 Choose an answer
Copy and complete this sentence, choosing the correct ending from the list below.

Organisms show variation. This means that

they reproduce in their habitats
they all have characteristics
they belong to a species
they are all slightly different

2 True or false?
Decide whether the following statements are true or false. Write down the true ones. Correct the false ones before you write them down.
a Nocturnal animals are active at night.
b Diurnal animals are active at night.
c Building up food stores and sleeping through the winter is called habitation.
d Migration allows birds to avoid climatic stress.

3 Predators and prey
Match up each adaptation with the correct reason below, and then write a complete sentence. Underline them in orange if they describe predators, and in blue if they describe prey. Draw a cartoon predator animal (orange) and a cartoon prey animal (blue).

Adaptations
Eyes at the front of the head mean they
Eyes on the sides of the head mean they
Sharp teeth, claws or beak are good
Camouflage allows them to
They are fast and strong so they are
They are fast and easily startled so they are

Reasons
blend into the background so they are not noticed.
can judge distances and catch moving animals.
for killing the prey and tearing it apart.
good at hunting.
can watch for danger all around.
good at escaping.

4 Food adaptations
Four adaptations are listed below. For each one, write a sentence saying what sort of food you think the animal might eat. Suggest what the animal might be.
o long neck, flat teeth
o strong jaw muscles, large pointed teeth
o thick strong beak
o small thin beak

5 Food chains and webs
Use the following information to draw three separate food chains. Colour code them to show producers and consumers. Then link them together in a food web.

Slugs eat lettuces.
Thrushes eat slugs.
Sparrowhawks eat thrushes.
Rabbits eat lettuces.
Foxes eat rabbits.
Sparrowhawks eat rabbits.
Rabbits eat grass.

6 Mind map
Draw a mind map for this topic using the following words. Add more words where you want.

environments	producers
habitats	prey
environmental conditions	predators
changing conditions	herbivores
adaptations	carnivores
organisms	omnivores
variation	food chains
feeding relationships	food webs
consumers	

Variation and classification

Before starting this unit, you should already be familiar with these ideas from earlier work.

○ By looking at the features of organisms, we can group together organisms that are similar. For animals found in a field, we might make two groups: those with legs and those without. Suggest some other features of animals you might look at in order to put them in groups.

○ We can identify different living things by looking at pictures and descriptions in books. Another method is by working through a series of questions. What is the name for a series of questions like this?

You will meet these key ideas as you work through this unit. Have a quick look now, and at the end of the unit read through them slowly.

○ All organisms are different – they show **variation**. They have different **characteristics**. Some characteristics are inherited from parents, and others depend on the environment.

○ Organisms that are very similar are grouped as a **species**. Humans are one species, dogs are another, and crocuses are another. Members of a species can breed together to produce fertile offspring.

○ Members of a species are similar, but they still show some variation. For example, all dogs have four legs, but they come in lots of shapes, sizes, colours and personalities.

○ We put organisms that are similar into groups. We usually start with two big main groups, plants and animals, and these are divided many times into smaller groups.

○ There are lots of animal groups. **Invertebrate** animals do not have a backbone. Jellyfish, earthworms, snails, starfish and spiders are all in different invertebrate groups.

○ **Vertebrate** animals have a backbone. Fish, frogs, snakes, birds and chimpanzees are all in different vertebrate groups.

Similar but different

○ **How do individuals of the same species differ from each other?**

All human beings belong to the same **species** (*Homo sapiens*). All dogs belong to the species (*Canis familiaris*). Members of the same species have similar characteristics and can breed together to produce **fertile** offspring (offspring that can also breed).

Look around you. Everyone in your class is different. Although we belong to the same species, characteristics such as eye and hair colour, height, weight, and shape of nose, differ from one person to the next. We call the differences between members of the same species **variation**. Members of different species, like humans and dogs, show even greater differences.

The pug and the great dane show variation but belong to the same species.

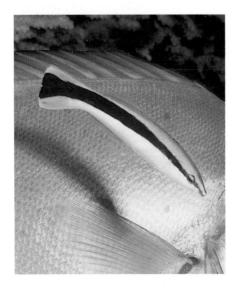

The cleaner wrasse (Labroides dimidiatus) and the blenny (Asidontus taeniatus) look the same but are different species.

Guess what?

Some species mimic others! The cleaner wrasse performs an important job in coral reef habitats – it cleans the bodies of other fish by nibbling away any parasites. The blenny has adapted to look and behave like a cleaner wrasse, but instead of removing parasites, it feeds on bits of other fish like their skin and fins!

Variation within a species

Members of the same species can vary in many ways. You could carry out an investigation to find out how a feature like hand span varies in your class. You could record your results in a table or spreadsheet.

hand span

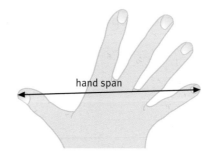

name	hand span (cm)
Vinay	13.7
Katie	12.1
Aliya	12.9
Jack	12.5

After sorting this data you could draw a graph to give a clear picture of how hand span varies:

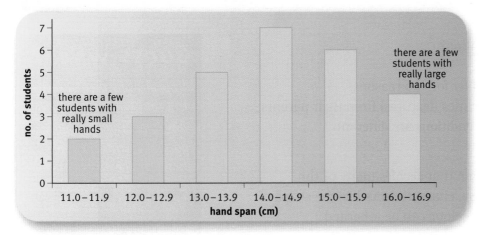

In science you'll often hear questions like, 'Is smoking linked to cancer?' (we know the answer to that one).

To find out if there really is a link between things we can use **data** (results) from investigations. For example, you might want to see if there's a link between hand span and height in your class:

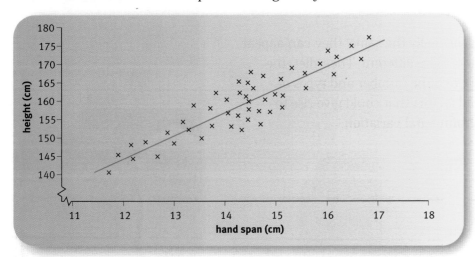

So does that mean that having big hands makes you tall?

A straight line has been drawn through the middle of the crosses – a **line of best fit**. We say that there's a **correlation** between hand span and height.

1 Copy and complete using words from the Language bank: A species is a set of _____ that can mate or _____ to produce offspring. Individual members of a species show _____ but members of different species show the biggest differences.

2 Explain the link between hand span and height in your own words.

3 Investigate the link between certain characteristics of another species. Start by asking a question like, 'Do pink-tipped daisies have longer stems?'

Language bank

breed
conclusion
correlation
line of best fit
offspring
organisms
reproduce
species
spreadsheet
variation

What are the causes of variation?

Individuals of the same species differ for two reasons:
○ they **inherit** different characteristics (features) from their parents;
○ their living or **environmental conditions** are different.

Inherited variation

Parents pass on genetic information that decides many of the characteristics of their children. So, **characteristics** like the shape of your nose and ears and your hair colour can be inherited.

When a sperm and an egg join, the two parents' genetic information mixes, giving a mixture of their characteristics to their children. Children are therefore **similar** to their parents but not identical. Different children of the same parents usually inherit a different mix of characteristics. This is what is known as **inherited variation**.

Environmental variation

Even though identical twins are genetically the same, they can appear very different if their living conditions are different. Their diet, the quality of health care they receive, and the number and types of illnesses they may have had, are all factors that could give rise to differences. This is known as **environmental variation**.

Twins' finger prints – similar but not identical.

Some characteristics, like height, are a combination of both inherited and environmental influences.

Twin	Carly	Katie	
Size feet	6	5	
Birthmark	on head	on back	
Height	150.5 cm	152.5 cm	
Supports	Man United	Barrow AFC	

Guess what?

Identical twins aren't exactly identical, even though they have come from the same egg and sperm. They will always be the same sex and have the same eye and hair colour. But they do not have identical fingerprints. Their fingerprints will be similar, but not exactly the same, because they will have been affected by environmental differences inside and outside the womb. So the police can use fingerprints to identify people – even identical twins.

As twins get older, they may begin to show greater differences. This is because the environment has had more time to affect them.

Identical twins show environmental variation.

Investigating variation

Selwyn grows tomatoes in his greenhouse, but he'd also like to grow them outside on his land in Yorkshire. He has four areas where he could grow them. Each gets a different amount of light and water and some have different soil types. To test which of the **environmental conditions** would be best for his plants, he germinated some seeds one spring. He placed 20 identical young tomato plants in each of the four areas with the differing conditions.

	Greenhouse	A	B	C	D
Conditions	light water good soil	dull light water good soil	light water good soil	light water very sandy soil	light little water good soil
Average height after 1 month (cm)	125	92	115	65	45

Conclusion: The growth of the tomato plants was affected by the light, water and soil conditions – that is, the environmental conditions in which they were growing. Of the outdoor areas, Area B produced the tallest plants.

Plants and animals will always develop according to the characteristics they inherit (hereditary characteristics) and the surroundings they live in. But plants are often influenced more than animals by small changes in their environment.

Tomatoes are affected by the smallest differences in growing conditions.

1 Copy and complete using words from the Language bank: Individual members of a species of plant or animal show _____. Variation may be _____ (which means it comes from the parents) or _____ (which means it comes from the organism's living conditions).

2 Carly and Katie are identical twins. List five ways they will be similar and five ways they may be different.

3 What kind of variation did Selwyn's tomatoes show?

4 How do you think Selwyn's tomato investigation could have been improved?

Language bank

characteristics
conditions
environmental
features
genetic
hereditary
inherited
variation

How can we describe living things?

Since ancient times people have taken an interest in the plants and animals around them. Some have described their feelings or **observations** (what they have seen) in poems and novels.

Caterpillar, *a poem by Norman MacCaig*

He stands on the suckers under his tail,
stretches forward and puts down
his six legs. Then he brings up
the sucker under his tail, making
a beautiful loop.

That's his way of walking. He makes
a row of upside-down U's
along the rib of a leaf. He is as green
as it.

The ways of walking! – horse, camel,
snail, me, crab, rabbit –
all inventing a way of journeying
till they become like the green caterpillar
that now stands on his tail
on the very tip of the leaf and sways, sways
like a tiny charmed snake,
groping in empty space for a foothold
where none is, where there is no
foothold at all.

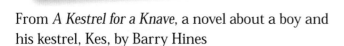

From *A Kestrel for a Knave*, a novel about a boy and his kestrel, Kes, by Barry Hines

[*Come on Kes*] and she came, head first, wings closed swooping down, hurtling down towards Billy, who waited, then lured her – whoosh – up, throwing up, ringing up, turning: and as she stooped again Billy twirled the lure and threw it high into her path. She caught it, and clutched it down to the ground.

Scientists also record their observations, which give us useful information about the appearance and behaviour of living organisms. We can find this kind of information in field guides and textbooks, on CD ROMs and videos, or on the Internet.

From the Collins Gem Guide: *Birds*

Nightingale
(*Luscinia megahynchos*)

This small brown bird has a coppery tail and is largely a summer resident in the east and south of England. Its habit of skulking in dense cover, this inconspicuous bird would be rarely noticed were it not for its liquid, bubbling, superbly warbled song.

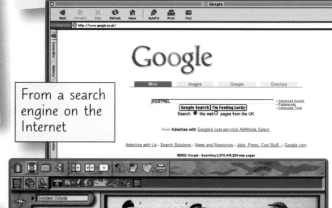

From a search engine on the Internet

From a CD-ROM

Your observations

Imagine you are a scientist. You might record your observations in a table, or on a labelled diagram. The number of legs and number of body sections are sometimes useful ways of sorting and identifying animals.

Recorded in a table:

	Number of legs	Number of body sections
Snail	none	1
Earthworm	none	many
Fish	none	1
Hamster	4	1
Ant	6	3
Spider	8	2

Recorded on a labelled diagram:

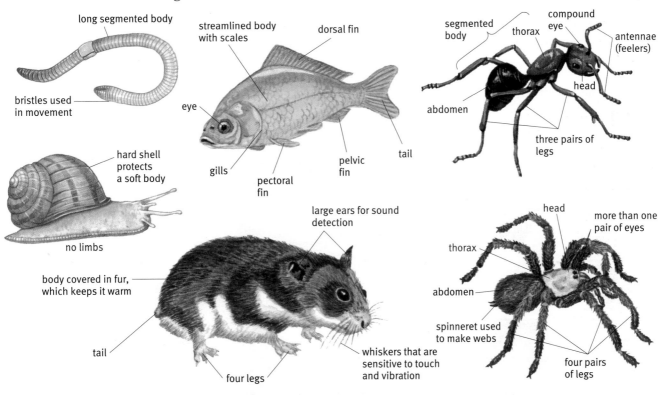

long segmented body
bristles used in movement
hard shell protects a soft body
no limbs

streamlined body with scales
dorsal fin
eye
gills
pectoral fin
pelvic fin
tail

segmented body
thorax
compound eye
antennae (feelers)
head
abdomen
three pairs of legs

large ears for sound detection
body covered in fur, which keeps it warm
tail
four legs
whiskers that are sensitive to touch and vibration

head
more than one pair of eyes
thorax
abdomen
spinneret used to make webs
four pairs of legs

1 Which source gives you most information about the appearance of the animals?

2 Which source tells the reader most about how the animal makes the writer feel?

3 Why are so many books and stories written about plants and animals.

4 Can poetry contain scientific information?

5 Name four differences between insects and spiders.

Language bank

abdomen
fins
head
observations
tail
thorax
wings

○ How can we sort things into groups?

A species is a group of living things that have similar characteristics. Sorting living things into groups is called **classification**. Scientists have created a way of classifying all living things. This helps us understand our world.

Plant or animal?

The simplest way of sorting a group of living things is to ask yourself, 'Is it a plant or an animal?'

It is usually easy to decide whether something is a plant or an animal.
○ Most plants are green, because they contain the green pigment **chlorophyll**, which they need to **photosynthesise** (make food).
○ Plants can grow, but they can't move about in the way that most animals can.

Plants can then be divided into smaller groups. We call these groups **taxonomic** groups.

These plants produce seeds and fruit

bluebell

horse chestnut tree

Flowering plants

water lily

Non-flowering plants

conifer

Conifers produce seeds, are usually evergreen and keep their leaves in winter

moss

Ferns have roots, and leaves (fronds) produce spores

fern

liverwort

Mosses and liverworts have simple leaves but no roots

Backbone or not?

Animals can also be sorted into taxonomic groups. To sort out a group of animals, one of the first questions to ask is:

'Do they have a backbone or not?'

This divides any group of animal into **vertebrates** and **invertebrates**. Vertebrates have a backbone and invertebrates do not. The diagram below shows how animals can be classified into even smaller groups.

Invertebrates

Cnidarians
Sac-like body
Some have hard coating
Mostly marine (live in sea)

jellyfish

Flatworms
Long thin body
Live in soil, water or other animals
(these are parasites)

tapeworm

Roundworms
Long body with round cross- section
Live in soil or are parasites

Segmented worms
Long body split into rings or
segments
Live in water or are parasites

leech

Molluscs
Usually have a shell, soft body,
no segments
Aquatic or marine

snail

Echinoderms (spiny-skinned invertebrates)
Tough skin on body with five parts
Marine

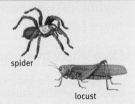
starfish

Arthropods
Hard outer skeleton (exoskeleton)
Have simple eyes and feelers
(Include arachnids and insects)

spider

locust

Vertebrates

Fish
Body covered in scales
Have gills
Live in water

shark

Amphibians
Soft skin with no scales
Have lungs
Lay eggs in water but live on land

newt

Reptiles
Skin tough and hard with scales
Have lungs
Lay eggs on land

python

Birds
Skin has feathers
Have lungs
Have wings for flying
Lay eggs

owl

Mammals
Skin has hair
Have lungs
Mother carries offspring inside
body until birth, after which
they feed off her milk

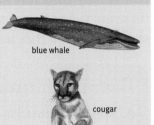
blue whale

cougar

Language bank

amphibian
animals
arthropod
characteristics
classification
cnidarian
invertebrates
mammal
mollusc
plants
reptile
species
vertebrates

1 Copy and complete using words from the Language bank: Living
things with similar _____ can be sorted into groups. There
are different ways of classifying living things. The two main groups
of living things are green _____ and animals. Animals can be
subdivided into _____ and invertebrates.

2 A newly discovered organism lays eggs on land and has hard scaly
skin. Place it into an appropriate taxonomic group.

3 Describe the main differences between a reptile and an amphibian.

4 List the main taxonomic groups used to classify animals and briefly
describe them.

How do scientists classify living things?

Classification is all about sorting organisms into groups. Simple classification involves observing and comparing organisms, but more detailed information, such as genetic make-up, is now used.

To simply classify living things we ask questions like:
Is it a plant or an animal?
Does it have a backbone?
How many legs does it have?
Does it have body segments or not?

Questions like Does it have wings? Does it live in water? Does it live on land or live in the air? Does it have legs, wings or neither? are not a particularly good way of dividing up living things. Using the answers to these questions, you may put birds, insects and flying lizards into the same group, but they are genetically very different.

I thought all animals were soft and fluffy.

No, animals include birds, spiders, humans... I could go on for hours!

Carolus Linnaeus

A Swedish naturalist called Carolus Linnaeus (1707–1778) was really the first to get to grips with **classification**. He classified plants and animals by dividing them into **taxonomic groups**.

In 1727 Linnaeus began studying medicine at the University of Lund, but still pursued his love of plants and continued to study botany.

In 1751 Linnaeus published *Philosophia Botanica*. This was a very important work because in it he introduced a way of naming organisms in Latin, which could be understood by people in different countries. For each species, he chose one general (**genus**) name and one specific (**species**) name. This provided a two-name system that could be used to label any living organism.

Today, living organisms are also classified according to genetic similarities – information that was not available in Linnaeus's day. But we still use his **binomial nomenclature** (a fancy way of saying 'two-name system') and every species still has a Latin name.

Here's how living organisms are grouped:

Kingdom	Animal	Plant
	human	stinging nettle
Phylum	Vertebrate	Angiosperm
Class	Mammal	Dicotyledon
Order	Primate	Urticales
Family	Hominid	Urticaceae
Genus	*Homo*	*Urtica*
Species	*sapiens*	*dioica*

The five kingdoms

All living things belong to one of five **kingdoms**. Plants and animals are two of these kingdoms.

Kingdom	Body's structural organisation	Method of nutrition	Examples	No. of known species (approx.)	Size and example
Prokaryotes	small, simple single cell (nucleus doesn't have a membrane); some form chains	absorb food	bacteria, blue-green algae, and spirochetes	10,000+	*1 µm (that's a thousandth of a mm)* bacterium
Protoctista	large, single cell (nucleus is enclosed by a membrane); some form chains or colonies	absorb, ingest (eat), and/or photosynthesise food	protozoans like amoeba and algae	250,000+	*1 mm* amoeba
Fungi	multicellular (many cells) thread-like organisms with specialised cells	absorb food	Pin mould, mushrooms, yeasts, mildews, and potato blight	100,000+	*6 cm* mushroom
Plants	multicellular form with specialised cells; do not have their own means of locomotion	photosynthesise	mosses, ferns, woody and non-woody flowering plants	250,000+	*few cm to many metres* oak tree
Animals	multicellular form with specialised cells have their own means of locomotion	ingest (eat) food	sponges, worms, insects, fish, amphibians, reptiles, birds, and mammals	millions	*few cm to several metres* hamster

1 Copy and complete using words from the Language bank: The Linnaean system of naming living things gives every _____ a two-part Latin name. This name is made up of the _____ and species names.

2 List the five kingdoms of the living world and briefly describe them.

3 Why is it sometimes difficult to tell which kingdom an organism belongs to?

4 Find out which genus and species the family dog belongs to.

Language bank

bacteria
class
family
fungi
genus
monera
multicellular
order
phylum (phyla)
protoctista
species
taxonomic group

Checkpoint

1 We are all different

Match up the beginnings and endings to make complete sentences. Use a different colour to write each sentence.

Beginnings

Variation means that organisms

Some different characteristics, such as different eye colours,

A scar is an example of

How fat you are

Endings

environmental variation.

is influenced by both inheritance and environment.

are inherited.

have different characteristics.

2 True or false?

Decide whether the following statements are true or false. Write down the true ones. Correct the false ones before you write them down.

a Alsatians and labradors can breed to form fertile offpring.

b Alsatians and labradors are different species.

c Alsatians and labradors do not show variation.

d Alsatians and labradors are mammals.

3 Identifying organisms

You have a daisy, a moss, a fern, a fly, an earthworm and a frog. Draw a simple key so that an alien can identify them. You could include the following questions.

Questions

Is it green?

Does it have flowers?

Does it have wings?

4 Inverted invertebrates

Match up the organisms and groups. Write a sentence for each one saying what features you used in order to decide which was which.

Organisms

snail

earthworm

crab

jellyfish

Invertebrate groups

arthropod

mollusc

cnidarian

segmented worm

5 Vertebrates

Copy and complete these sentences, filling in the vertebrate groups. Do a quick sketch of an animal from each group, either real or imaginary.

_____ have scales, breathe air, lay eggs on land.

_____ have scales, live in water, lay eggs in water.

_____ have hair, breathe air, live on land, feed young on milk.

_____ have feathers, breathe air, have wings, lay eggs on land.

_____ do not have scales, live in water and on land, lay eggs in water.

Acids and alkalis

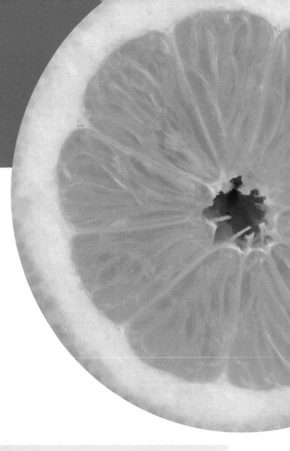

Before starting this unit, you should already be familiar with these ideas from earlier work.

○ Solids can dissolve and form solutions. Is this a reversible or irreversible change?

○ Sometimes when you mix materials, new materials are formed. What might you see to tell you that new materials were formed? Think about mixing lemon juice and bicarbonate of soda, for example.

You will meet these key ideas as you work through this unit. Have a quick look now, and at the end of the unit read through them slowly.

○ **Acids** and **alkalis** are two groups of chemicals. They each have their own properties and uses. Lemon juice is acidic, and soapy water is alkaline.

○ Acids and alkalis can be dangerous, so we must handle them carefully. Strong acids are **corrosive**.

○ We can describe solutions as **acidic**, **alkaline** or **neutral**. An **indicator** is a substance that changes colour to tell us whether a solution is acidic, alkaline or neutral.

○ The **pH scale** describes how acidic or alkaline a solution is. It is a scale from 0 to 14, with 0 being most acidic and 14 being most alkaline. 7 on the scale is neutral.

○ If we add enough alkali to an acid, the solution becomes neutral. A chemical change has happened, which is called a **chemical reaction**. This type of reaction is called a **neutralisation** reaction.

What are acids and alkalis like and where do we use them?

Have you ever sucked a lemon? Your mouth's probably watering, just thinking about it. Lemon juice contains **acid**, which is detected by the very back of your tongue. It's this **citric acid** that tastes so sour.

What are acids?

Some acids, like lemon juice and vinegar, are harmless and are often used to give foods a tangy flavour. These acids are **weak acids**. **Strong acids** are too dangerous to taste or touch. They can cause damage to skin, wood, cloth, and other materials by **corroding** them (wearing them away).

Lemons contain a weak solution of citric acid.

HAZARD

Never, never, never taste chemicals in the lab or at home.

We find acids in many foods, household products and toiletries.

What are alkalis?

Alkalis are another group of chemicals. They are the chemical opposite of acids. Some alkalis can be just as corrosive as acids, and are therefore also dangerous to taste and touch. We say that they are **caustic**. Alkalis are used in soaps and many household cleaning products. **Sodium hydroxide** is a particularly useful alkali that is used in making paper and soap, for example.

Guess what?

Ant bites contain a weak acid called **methanoic acid** (which used to be called formic acid). It is the acid in the ant bite that irritates your skin and causes pain.

Alkalis dissolve in water and make good cleaning materials.

Acids in your body

Some acids are found inside your body! For example, your stomach contains **hydrochloric acid**, which helps to digest your food.

Healthy skin is also naturally acidic. This acidity kills some bacteria that may come into contact with it. Some moisturising creams and gels are advertised as being 'pH balanced'. This means that they have a similar acidity to your skin.

This moisturising shower gel has a pH similar to that of skin.

Science in advertising

We have all seen adverts for shampoos and conditioners promising to 'energise', 'revitalise', 'nourish' or 'rejuvenate' our hair with some special new ingredient. The truth is that hair products cannot do any of these things because hair is not 'alive'. Hair is actually a strand of dead proteins. The outside layer of a hair is called the cuticle, which is made up of separate scales. If a conditioner is acidic the scales will smooth down, which may make hair look healthy.

A scanning electron micrograph of a hair, showing protein scales.

NEW *Vitalok* **shampoo and conditioner**

A unique formulation of vitamins and essential oils to nourish and add life to dull hair

enriched with **PRO-NUTRA**

1 Copy and complete using words from the Language bank: Acids and alkalis are groups of chemicals. Some acids are _____ and some alkalis are _____, so should be treated with care. Acids and alkalis are used in a range of everyday household products. Hair conditioners and some skin moisturisers are _____.

2 Which acid do lemons contain?

3 List some of the uses of acids and alkalis in the home.

4 Write the words 'acid' and 'alkali' on two separate lines in your workbook. Next to each one, write down the words from the list below that describe it.

corrosive; caustic; sour; in drain cleaner; in vinegar

Language bank

acid
acidic
acidity
alkali
caustic
citric acid
corrosive
hydrochloric acid
methanoic acid
sodium hydroxide

○ **What are acids and alkalis like and where do we use them?**

Acids and alkalis are also found in science laboratories and factories. Acids are used in making fertilisers, explosives, plastics, synthetic fabrics, paints, dyes, medicines, detergents, and many other chemicals. Alkalis are used in making soap, glass, paper and textiles.

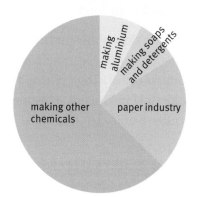

Some of the uses of sodium hydroxide.

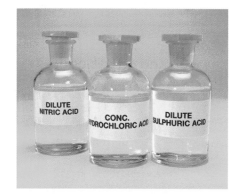

Acids that may be found in the laboratory.

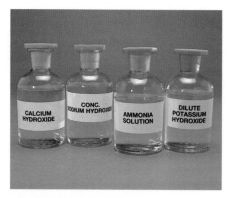

Alkalis that may be found in the laboratory.

Safety with acids and alkalis

So that we all know which chemicals are safe and which are dangerous, there is a set of signs called the **hazchem** system. These special symbols are put on containers and vehicles carrying dangerous chemicals, and explain why the chemical is dangerous. The system is international, so that the symbols can be understood by anyone in the world.

1 Explosive: Substance may explode if heated, knocked or ignited.

2 Irritant: Not corrosive but can cause blistering of the skin.

3 Harmful: Less dangerous than toxic but still dangerous.

4 Toxic: Serious health risk and could cause death. Could affect you if swallowed, breathed in or absorbed through the skin.

5 Radioactive: Gives off radiation. Treat like toxic.

6 Oxidising agent: May produce heat if it reacts with other chemicals. Can feed fires.

7 Corrosive: Destroys living tissue ('caustic' sometimes used for alkalis).

8 Highly flammable: May easily catch fire even under normal conditions.

Some chemicals, like nitric acid, really need more than one symbol. Nitric acid is corrosive, as well as being an oxidising agent.

Concentrated and dilute

If a large amount of an acid or an alkali is spilt, very often the fire brigade will hose the area with water.

The more water is mixed with an acid, the less **concentrated** and the more **dilute** the acid becomes. Dilute acids are less hazardous than concentrated acids.

At the same concentration, alkalis can actually be more hazardous than acids.

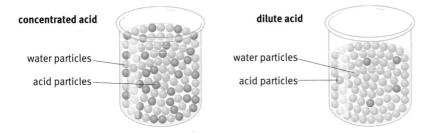

Concentrated and dilute solutions of acid.

Hazard! In the lab, never add water to an acid. Always add the acid to water. Some acids, like sulphuric acid, give out lots of heat when diluted. This can cause the water to boil off and it could splash into your face.

Acid or alkali spilt in the lab

If you spill or splash an acid or an alkali on yourself in the lab:
1 Wash the spill with lots of water for about 10 minutes.
2 If the spill is on the bench or floor, mop it up and then clean the area with water. In all cases, **tell the teacher** and **don't panic**.

1 Copy and complete using words from the Language bank: A series of signs and symbols called the _____ system helps us to recognise dangerous substances. If an _____ or _____ is spilt or splashed on the skin, plenty of cold water must be run over the splashed area. Mixing water with an acid or alkali solution _____ it and makes it less _____, or dangerous.

2 Name two things that are made with acids and two things that are made with alkalis.

3 What should you wear when using acids and alkalis in the lab?

4 Why is it important for lorries to carry information about the chemicals they are transporting?

So are alkalis dangerous too?

Yes, sometimes more dangerous than acids!

It is important to indicate which chemicals are being transported so the emergency services anywhere in the world can deal with accidents.

Language bank

acid
alkali
caustic
concentrated
corrosive
dilutes
explosive
harmful
hazard
hazardous
hazchem system
highly flammable
irritant
oxidising agent
radioactive
toxic

○ How can acids and alkalis be identified and distinguished from each other?
○ Is there a range of acidity and alkalinity?
○ What happens when an acid is added to an alkali?

One of these colourless liquids is an acid, but which one? They both look like water.

The way to tell whether a colourless liquid is an acid or an alkali is to use an **indicator**. An indicator contains a **dye** that changes colour depending on whether it is mixed with an acid or an alkali.

Plant dye and litmus indicators

We can make our own indicators using the dye from red cabbage, raw beetroot and blackcurrant. The plant is crushed with a mortar and pestle and the juice that comes out acts as the indicator.

Indicator/solution	Red cabbage	Raw beetroot	Blackcurrant	Acid or alkali?
Sodium hydroxide	green/yellow	yellow	green	alkali
Hydrochloric acid	pink/red	red/purple	red	acid

In the lab, red and blue litmus paper can be used to find out if a substance is acidic or alkaline.

Blue litmus paper goes red in acid and red litmus paper goes blue in alkali.

How acidic or how alkaline?

Litmus and plant dye indicators just tell us if something is **acidic** (contains an acid) or **alkaline** (contains an alkali).

Universal indicator (UI) is a mixture of many dyes. It tells us how acidic or alkaline a substance is. We measure the strength of acids and alkalis using the **pH scale**. On this scale of numbers from 0 to 14, acids have a pH of less than 7. The lower the pH, the stronger the acid. Alkalis have a pH of more than 7. The higher the pH, the stronger the alkali.

Universal indicator paper in weak and strong acid (left) and weak and strong alkali (right).

Universal indicator comes as a solution (above) or as paper (left).

The colour of the universal indicator tells us the pH of the substance.

pH 1   2   3   4   5   6   7   8   9   10   11   12   13   14

battery acid   lemon juice   wine   milk of magnesia   drain cleaner

	strong acid	weak acid	neutral	weak alkali	strong alkali
Lab examples	hydrochloric acid	ethanoic acid	water	ammonia solution	sodium hydroxide
Everyday examples	battery acid (sulphuric acid)	lemon juice (citric acid)	alcohol	milk of magnesia	drain cleaner

Substances with a very high or a very low pH are the most dangerous. An acid that is just one pH number lower than another acid is actually ten times stronger. Similarly, an alkali that is one pH number higher than another is ten times stronger than that alkali.

Neutralisation

A solution with a low pH can be made safe by adding a solution with a high pH to it. This brings the pH nearer to 7, which is **neutral**. An acid will **neutralise** an alkali, and an alkali will neutralise an acid. Neutralisation reactions give out heat, so care is needed.

The sting of the stinging nettle.

Guess what?

Nettle stings contain an acidic chemical that irritates the skin. Dock plants often grow near nettles and their leaves contain an alkali. If a dock leaf is rubbed on a nettle sting it helps to ease the pain by neutralising the acid.

1 Copy and complete using words from the Language bank: Dyes that change colour in the presence of an acid or an alkali are known as _____. _____ indicator gives a range of colours in acidic and alkaline solutions that can be matched to a pH. pH numbers indicate how _____ or alkaline a solution is. _____ solutions have a pH of 7, _____ solutions have a pH below 7 and _____ solutions have a pH above 7.

2 Name two common acids and two common alkalis.

3 What is universal indicator solution?

4 Describe how you would measure the pH of an unknown colourless solution.

5 Explain what is meant by neutralisation.

6 Describe two ways you could neutralise a solution of hydrochloric acid.

Language bank

acidic
alkaline
indicators
litmus paper
neutral
neutralise
pH
universal indicator

○ What happens when an acid is added to an alkali?
○ Where is neutralisation important?

When acids and alkalis are mixed, a chemical change occurs. We call this a **chemical reaction**. More specifically, we call it a neutralisation reaction, because the pH of the mixture gets closer to 7.

Using alkali on acid

Some people have too much acid in their stomach, which causes indigestion. They take **antacids** to help remove this excess acid. The antacids contain an alkali, which **neutralises** some of the acid.

Some plants do not grow properly in soil that is too acidic. Farmers use an alkali called lime (calcium hydroxide) to neutralise acidic soil.

When the right amounts of an acid and an alkali are added together a neutral solution is obtained.

A well-known antacid.

Getting the pH of the soil right for crops is very important.

Guess what?

In the mid-1700s, an Italian scientist called Lazzaro Spallanzani investigated the contents of his stomach. He would swallow sponges on a string and then pull them back up to examine the acidic contents. He concluded that the stomach contains hydrochloric acid.

pull

Acid rain

Gases from factories and power stations and exhaust fumes from cars, form weak acids in the atmosphere. These acids fall to the ground in rain or snow. This is called **acid rain**. Acid rain damages buildings, kills trees and plants, and pollutes water. Some lakes in Scandinavia have been treated with calcium carbonate, which neutralises the acidity and helps to protect the wildlife.

Chemicals are sprayed into a lake to neutralise the effects of acid rain.

Making a fertiliser

When ammonium hydroxide (an alkali) and nitric acid are mixed together there is a neutralisation reaction. Ammonium nitrate is made in the reaction. This is an important **fertiliser**.

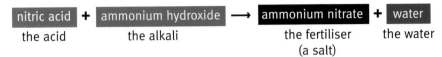

| nitric acid | + | ammonium hydroxide | → | ammonium nitrate | + | water |
| the acid | | the alkali | | the fertiliser (a salt) | | the water |

The salt is a fertiliser, as it helps to provide plants with nitrogen. Nitrogen is an important element, which plants use to make proteins.

pH probes in neutralisation reactions

Universal indicator solution gives us the pH of a solution as a whole number. But the pH scale is a **continuous** scale, which means that there could be pH values between the whole numbers – of, say, 3.7 or 9.1. **pH probes** can be used to measure the pH of a solution when an exact or continuous measurement of pH is needed, like in the example below.

The probe reads the pH and the **data logger** processes the information, and then sends it to the computer. Software plots the data as a graph. The graph shows how the pH of the acid changes as alkali is added.

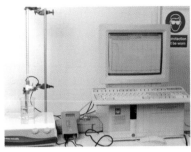

Data logging is just a way of recording readings or data electronically.

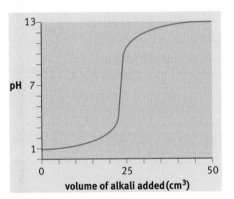

The changes in pH as sodium hydroxide is added to hydrochloric acid.

When sodium hydroxide (NaOH) was added to hydrochloric acid (HCl), this curve was obtained. The centre of the vertical part of the graph is the point of neutralisation. Because more alkali is added than is needed to neutralise the acid, the curve ends at an alkaline pH.

1 Copy and complete using words from the Language bank:
   Neutralisation reactions produce _____ solutions, which means that the pH is 7. Some neutralisation reactions are used to produce important chemicals, such as _____ nitrate.

2 Why is it important to reduce acidity in polluted lakes?

3 What are fertilisers and why are they useful?

4 Find out the chemical formula of hydrochloric acid, sulphuric acid and nitric acid.

5 Why do you think sodium hydroxide is not used to neutralise acidic lakes?

Language bank

acid rain
ammonium hydroxide
ammonium nitrate
antacid
chemical reaction
data logger
fertiliser
neutral
neutralisation reaction
nitric acid
nitrogen
pH probe

Checkpoint

1 Acid or alkali?

Classify each of these substances as an acid or alkali. Write two lists, acids in red and alkalis in blue. Add any more examples you can think of. You could draw a sketch of each.

Substances

cola

oven cleaner

orange juice

vinegar

bleach

moisturiser

indigestion medicine

soap

lemon juice

2 Safety first

Copy and complete these sentences, unscrambling the words.

a Some acids and alkalis can cause blisters on the skin. They are **snittarir**.

b **Uhlmarf** chemicals are not as dangerous as toxic ones, but you still need to be careful with them.

c **Visorcore** materials can burn holes in you!

d Nitric acid is **gixidison** as well as being corrosive.

3 True or false?

Decide whether the following statements are true or false. Write down the true ones. Correct the false ones before you write them down.

a Strong alkalis might have a pH of 1.

b Strong acids might have a pH of 1.

c A solution with a pH of 7 is described as natural.

d Universal indicator tells us the pH of a solution.

4 Choose the answer

Copy and complete this sentence, choosing the correct ending.

If you mix equal volumes of an acid and an alkali at the same strength, the solution will be

red.

neutral.

bubbling.

caustic.

5 Litmus test

Match up the beginnings and endings to make complete sentences.

Beginnings

If you put red litmus paper in acid,

If you put red litmus paper in alkali,

If you put blue litmus paper in acid,

If you put blue litmus paper in alkali,

Endings

it will go red.

it will stay red.

it will go blue.

it will stay blue.

Simple chemical reactions

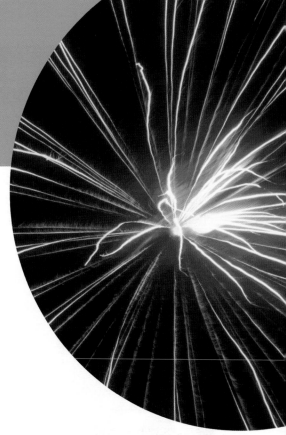

Before starting this unit, you should already be familiar with these ideas from earlier work.

○ Some substances are normally gases, such as oxygen. Think of as many other gases as you can.
○ In irreversible changes, new materials are formed. Irreversible changes cannot easily be changed back. Can you think of an irreversible change in cooking?

You will meet these key ideas as you work through this unit. Have a quick look now, and at the end of the unit read through them slowly.

○ In a **chemical reaction**, new materials are formed. These are different from the materials we started with. When a chemical reaction happens we often see a change, such as bubbles, a colour change, or a solid being formed. The reaction might give off heat, or even produce a flame.
○ When an acid reacts with a metal, the gas **hydrogen** is formed. For example, hydrochloric acid reacts with magnesium to give bubbles. A **salt** is formed as well – it's magnesium chloride in this reaction.
○ When an acid reacts with a carbonate, **carbon dioxide** gas is formed. For example, calcium carbonate reacts with hydrochloric acid and you see bubbles. A **salt** (calcium chloride) and **water** are also formed in the reaction.
○ For a material to burn, we need **oxygen**. When things burn, they react with oxygen in the air and form **oxides**.
○ We use **word equations** to represent reactions. The **reactants** are on the left, and the **products** are on the right.

○ What is a chemical reaction?

Everything in the universe is made up of **material**. Some materials like gold or copper are used as we find them. Many materials need a **chemical change** before we can use them. A chemical change involves a **chemical reaction**.

'Material' does not just mean 'fabric' or 'cloth'.

Both of these processes involve a chemical reaction.

Melting and boiling are physical changes. No new substances are made, and the changes are easy to reverse. In chemical changes, new substances are made, and the changes are usually difficult to reverse.

The materials that are changed are called **reactants** and what they change into are called **products**.

go to

reactants ⟶ products

We show what happens in a chemical reaction in a word **equation**. The equation always shows what chemicals are reacting in the reaction and what they make – the products.

For example:

1 Chemical reactions often happen in cooking:

ingredients (reactants) → cake (product)

flour + baking powder + sugar + butter + eggs ⟶ cake

2 Some chemical reactions involve explosions:

hydrogen + oxygen ⟶ water

Wax melting is a physical change – a change that is easy to reverse because when liquid wax cools it turns back to solid wax.

Guess what?
The chemical name for water is dihydrogen monoxide!

The products have different **properties** from the reactants (they may look or behave differently). For example, water is very different from hydrogen and oxygen.

Material	Properties
Hydrogen	gas – explosive
Oxygen	gas – supports burning
Water	liquid – non-flammable; used to put fires out

How to spot a chemical reaction

There are certain signs we can look for that tell us that something has undergone a chemical reaction. The table below lists some of the words or phrases you could use to describe a reaction.

What happens	Words used to describe chemical reaction	
It fizzes or bubbles are given off (sometimes you can smell the gas).	gas evolves or effervesces	
It feels warm or the temperature goes up.	heat emitted	
The reaction glows or a flame is produced.	light emitted	
Small particles (usually carbon) are made, which get finely spread out through the air.	smoke produced	
A solid forms in a solution and sinks to the bottom.	precipitate produced	
The colour changes.	colour change	

1 Copy and complete using words from the Language bank: A chemical change involves a chemical _____. This is a permanent change and a new material with new properties is made. A _____ _____is a short way of writing what happens in a chemical reaction.

2 In the following reactions, which substances are the reactants and what is the product?
   a potassium nitrate + sulphur → gunpowder
   b magnesium + oxygen → magnesium oxide

3 When ice melts and becomes water, has a chemical change taken place? Explain your answer.

Language bank

chemical change
chemical reaction
effervesces
hydrogen
material
oxygen
precipitate
products
properties
reactants
word equation

Reactions of acids

○ How do acids react with metals?
○ How do acids react with carbonates?

Some acids are described as **corrosive** because they eat away some materials. Corrosion is a chemical reaction.

Do all metals react with acid in the same way?

Look at the pictures below. They show how some metals react with **hydrochloric acid**.

Zinc reacting with hydrochloric acid.

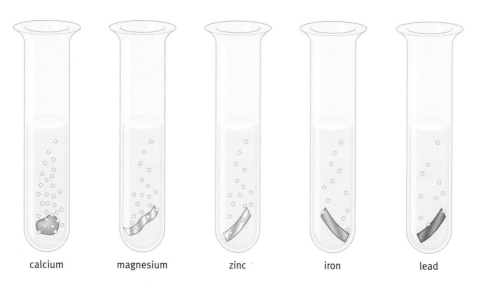

| calcium | magnesium | zinc | iron | lead | copper | silver |

Some of the metals get smaller and seem to disappear. Bubbles are given off. The metals don't disappear, of course, they simply change into the products of the **corrosion** reaction – a **salt** and **hydrogen**.

Some other metals don't do anything at all – they don't react with the acid.

Testing the gas

Bubbles of gas are produced when a metal reacts with an acid. It's a **flammable** gas (it burns), which makes a squeaky pop when a flame is brought near to it. This shows that it's hydrogen.

The **lighted splint ('squeaky pop')** test for hydrogen:

1 Wearing goggles, collect a tube of hydrogen gas in an upturned test tube.

2 Light a wooden splint.

3 Remove the stopper and place the splint next to the mouth of the test tube.

4 The gas should ignite with a loud squeaky pop.

Getting to know hydrogen

Colour – colourless

Odour – odourless

Litmus – neutral

Density – much less than air

Solubility in water – not soluble

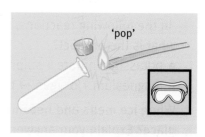

The squeaky pop test confirms that the gas is hydrogen.

Reactions of acids with carbonates

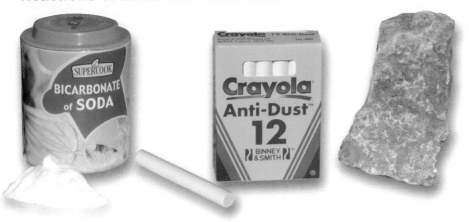

Common carbonates: bicarbonate of soda (sodium hydrogencarbonate), chalk, and limestone (both calcium carbonate).

Carbonates are chemicals that contain carbon and oxygen. Acids react with carbonates like calcium carbonate (chalk) and sodium hydrogencarbonate. The carbonates seem to disappear, but in fact change into **a salt**, **water** and **carbon dioxide gas**. The bubbles that you see are carbon dioxide.

carbonate + acid → salt + water + carbon dioxide

Sodium hydrogencarbonate (bicarbonate of soda) reacting with hydrochloric acid.

The test for carbon dioxide

Carbon dioxide stops things burning, so if a splint is lit and put into a tube of carbon dioxide, the flame goes out.

A better way to find out if a colourless gas is carbon dioxide is called the **limewater test**. When carbon dioxide is passed through limewater, the liquid goes cloudy.

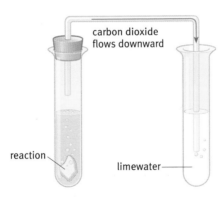

carbon dioxide flows downward

reaction

limewater

Getting to know carbon dioxide

Colour – colourless

Odour – odourless

Litmus – acidic in water

Density – greater than air

Solubility in water – soluble

Language bank ○—

carbon dioxide
carbonates
corrode
corrosive
density
flammable
hydrochloric acid
hydrogen
lighted splint ('squeaky pop') test
limewater
litmus
odour
salt
solubility

1 Copy and complete using words from the Language bank: Acids react with most metals to make a _____ and _____ gas. In the _____ splint test hydrogen makes a _____ _____ noise. _____ react with acids to make a salt, water and carbon dioxide. _____ goes cloudy in the presence of carbon dioxide.

2 What makes the fizz in fizzy drinks?

3 Why is carbon dioxide used in some fire extinguishers?

4 Why do you think recipes for blackcurrant jam recommend that you boil the fruit in pans made from copper or glass, and not iron?

Burning things

○ **What new substances are made when materials burn in air or oxygen?**

Air contains a mixture of gases, mainly **oxygen** and **nitrogen**. Oxygen is an important gas – we need it to stay alive and it's essential for **burning** to take place.

A burning question!

Burning is a chemical reaction. When things burn, they react with oxygen to make **oxides**, and heat and light are released. Burning is also known as **combustion**.

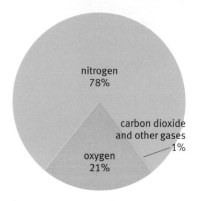

The composition of air.

Sulphur burns vigorously in pure oxygen, but it is important to follow the safety rules carefully.

The word equation for sulphur burning is:

sulphur + oxygen ⟶ sulphur dioxide

The **fire triangle** shows that **heat**, a **fuel**, and **oxygen** are needed to make something burn. A fuel is anything that can burn. If just one of these is removed, then a fire will go out.

Firefighters use this knowledge to put out fires. They can:
○ cool things down with water, which removes the **heat**;
○ smother a fire with foam, which removes the **oxygen**;
○ let it burn out, which removes the **fuel**.

Getting to know oxygen

Colour – colourless

Odour – odourless

Litmus – neutral

Density – about the same as air

Solubility in water – quite soluble in water

Other facts: Oxygen freezes solid at −218 °C. That's 218 °C below zero!

A fire needs something to burn, oxygen and heat.

1 If a candle is burnt under a bell jar the candle goes out. Why? The candle needs oxygen to burn and this becomes used up. How do we know?

2 If the candle is put on a dish and floated in water the candle goes out. The water rises up the jar to take the place of the oxygen used up.

3 The water rises about one-fifth $\left(\frac{1}{5}\right)$ of the way up the jar, as about one-fifth of the air is oxygen (well 21% to be exact). The other gases in the air like nitrogen and carbon dioxide are not used up in combustion. This is why the water doesn't fill the jar completely.

Fire prevention

The home is the most likely place for a fire to start. The fire services recommend a number of common sense 'dos' and 'don'ts' to prevent a fire at home.

Look at the house in the picture. It's just packed full of potential fire hazards. People could get seriously hurt here. How many hazards can you find?

Don't do this at home!

1 Copy and complete using words from the Language bank: Burning is also known as _____. It is a chemical reaction in which a material reacts with _____ to produce an _____, releasing heat and light.

2 What three things are needed to make something burn?

3 Draw and label all the apparatus someone would use to burn sulphur safely in the lab.

4 Why do you think you need to take extra care if substances are burnt in oxygen rather than just air?

5 Design and make a small information leaflet that explains to young children the key points about fire safety. Give it a good title, like 'Fire safety – get it right!'.

Language bank

carbon dioxide
combustion
fire triangle
fuel
nitrogen
oxide
oxygen
sulphur

71

○ What is produced when fuels burn?
○ What is needed for things to burn?

A fuel is something that burns to produce useful energy, like heat and light. Fuels store **chemical energy**, which is released as heat and light energy when they burn.

Guess what?

There's a quick way of writing down the names of chemicals: carbon dioxide is CO_2 and water is H_2O.

Fuels release energy when they are burned.

Petrol

Paraffin

Natural gas (mainly methane)

Wax

Wood

Butane and propane

Many everyday fuels, such as coal, oil and natural gas, are what we call **fossil fuels**. Fossil fuels are the remains of plants and animals that died millions of years ago.

Fossil fuels are made up mainly of carbon and hydrogen, so when they burn, they make the oxides of carbon and hydrogen. We call these carbon dioxide and water.

Methane

Methane is the main ingredient of the natural gas that burns in our gas fires and gas hobs at home. It's a fossil fuel.

> I know about fossils – they are made of stone.

> Not fossil fuels mate. They can be solids, like coal, or liquid, or gas.

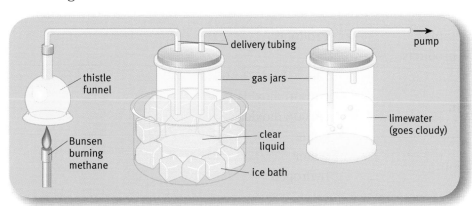

delivery tubing
pump
thistle funnel
gas jars
Bunsen burning methane
clear liquid
ice bath
limewater (goes cloudy)

The products made when methane burns are drawn through the apparatus.

Results	First container	Second container
Observations	colourless liquid seen	limewater goes cloudy
Inference (conclusion)	could be water	carbon dioxide present

We could check that the colourless liquid is water by seeing if it boils at 100 °C, or by checking if it turns blue cobalt chloride paper pink.

The overall reaction for methane burning is:

methane + oxygen → water + carbon dioxide

1 Copy and complete using words from the Language bank: A fuel is a substance that releases useful _____ when it burns, like heat and light. Fuels need _____ to burn. _____ _____ is produced when fuels that have carbon in them burn.

2 Name three fuels and say what they are used for.

3 Complete the word equation that summarises what happens when methane burns in air:

methane + oxygen ⟶ c_____ d_____ + w_____

4 Find out examples of when burning is used to celebrate things. What is burned? What is celebrated?

5 When methane burns, energy is released as heat and light. Do you think energy weighs anything? Explain your answer.

Language bank

carbon
carbon dioxide
chemical energy
energy
fossil fuel
hydrogen
methane
natural gas
oxygen

Checkpoint

1 Reactions happen

Match up the beginnings and endings to make complete sentences. Use a different colour to write each sentence.

Beginnings

A chemical reaction is an example of a

Freezing is an example of a

The substances that react, the reactants,

The substances that are made, the products,

Endings

are on the left of the word equation.

temporary change.

permanent change.

are on the right of the word equation.

2 True or false?

Decide whether the following statements are true or false. Write down the true ones. Correct the false ones before you write them down.

a Oxygen is a colourless gas with a strong smell of fish that supports burning.

b Hydrogen is a colourless odourless gas which is explosive.

c Carbon dioxide is a red gas which turns limewater pink.

d Water vapour is a colourless odourless gas which can be detected with cobalt chloride paper.

3 Reactions

Milly carried out three reactions:

a metal with acid

b carbonate with acid

c burning methane.

She mixed up her notes. For each reaction, choose the correct reactants, products and test for any gas produced. Write each reaction's notes in a different colour.

Reactants

methane

metal

carbonate

acid

acid

oxygen

Products

salt

salt

carbon dioxide

carbon dioxide

water

water

hydrogen

Tests

turns blue cobalt chloride paper pink (water does this)

squeaky pop

turns limewater cloudy

4 Put that fire out

Copy the fire triangle. Write on it what you could use to remove each side and put the fire out.

Particle model of solids, liquids and gases

Before starting this unit, you should already be familiar with these ideas from earlier work.

○ Solids, liquids and gases behave differently. Liquids have a fixed volume, and take up the shape of the bottom of their container. Does a solid have a fixed volume? What about a gas?

○ Solids can turn into liquids and liquids into gases, and back again. Can you draw a flow chart to show these changes of state? Add 'melting', 'boiling', 'freezing', 'condensing' over or under the arrows.

○ Changes of state can change back. What do we call this kind of change?

You will meet these key ideas as you work through this unit. Have a quick look now, and at the end of the unit read through them slowly.

○ The **particle model** says that matter is made up of basic units called **particles**.

○ In **solids** the particles are regularly arranged and touching.

○ In **liquids** the particles are randomly arranged but they are touching.

○ In **gases** the particles are randomly arranged and far apart, with large spaces between them. Because of the big spaces, gases do not conduct heat, and you can squash a gas.

○ The particles in matter are always moving. In a solid they vibrate. In a liquid they move faster. In a gas they move about quickly in all directions.

○ When you heat matter, you give the particles energy. They move more quickly. This pushes the particles apart, and the matter expands.

○ There are attractions between the particles in matter. These **forces of attraction** are strongest in solids, and weaker in liquids. There are no forces of attraction between the particles in gases.

○ Because the particles in liquids and gases can move about, they **diffuse**. This means they spread out and mix. Gases diffuse faster than liquids.

○ The particles in a gas move about so quickly that they are always bumping into each other and into the sides of their container. This creates **gas pressure**. The air exerts a pressure on us all the time, and we call this **air pressure**.

How can we explain evidence from experiments?

We know that if we took an object and split it in half, then in half again and again...eventually we would get to some kind of basic unit we call a **particle**. Like a house is made of bricks, matter is made of small things called particles. Matter can be a solid, a liquid or a gas.

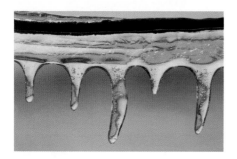
Solid

Liquid

Gas

How do we tell if matter is a solid, a liquid or a gas? Ask yourself some testing questions, like those below, and note down your observations.

1 Does it squash easily?

Most solids are hard to squash. So are liquids. But gases are easily squashed. They are easy to **compress**.

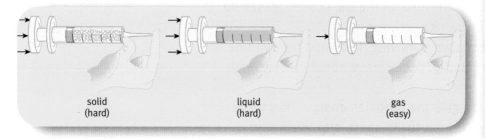

solid (hard)   liquid (hard)   gas (easy)

2 Does it help heat transfer?

Some solids are metals, like the bar in the pictures below. These **conduct** (transfer) heat well. Liquids and gases are not good conductors.

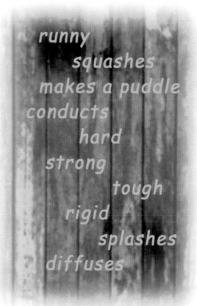

Words that can be used to describe solids, liquids and gases.

runny
squashes
makes a puddle
conducts
hard
strong
tough
rigid
splashes
diffuses

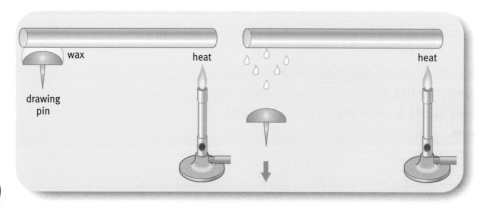

wax   heat   heat

drawing pin

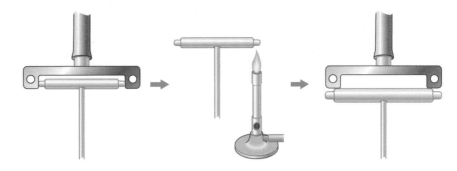

3 Does it expand (get bigger) on heating?

When a metal bar is heated it gets longer, and this is usually easy to measure. In fact, all states of matter **expand** on heating, but it can be harder to notice for liquids and gases. Some thermometers work because the alcohol in them expands. You might notice that your bike tyres get harder as the air in them warms up on hot days.

4 Does it diffuse (spread out)?

a Particles can **diffuse** (spread out) through liquids and gases. The solid crystals dissolve in the water and slowly spread out to give an even colour. They do this more quickly in hot water, so particles must move more quickly and have more energy in the hot water.

b You can smell the scent of perfume as soon as you open the bottle. Even holding perfume at arm's length, you can smell the vapour.

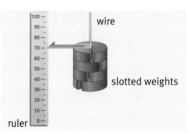

5 Does it stretch?

The length of the solid wire on the right is related to how many slotted weights are added (until it breaks).

6 How heavy is it – for its size?

Density tells us how much mass is packed into a certain space.

Both blocks have the same volume but their mass is different so their density is different. Solids are usually denser than liquids, and liquids are denser than gases.

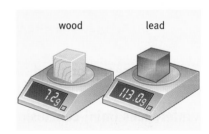

1 Copy and complete the table:

Will it...	solid	liquid	gas
squash	no		yes
conduct (heat)			
expand			
diffuse	no		
stretch			no
have high density	yes		

2 Put the words *density*, *dense* and *denser* into three different sentences so that the meaning of each is clear.

3 Draw a solid, a liquid and a gas, showing what you think the arrangement of particles in each might look like.

Language bank

compress
conduct
density
diffuse
expand
gas
liquid
particle
solid
squash
stretch

How are theories created?

If you've ever watched a murder mystery on TV, you'll know that bit by bit you uncover evidence that leads to a conclusion about which suspect carried out the murder.

In Science, you do **experiments** and **investigations** in which you might have made a **prediction**. This can lead to **observations** and **results** that may tell you something. This 'something' then leads to a **conclusion** that may confirm or make a new **theory**.

A theory is an idea that explains observations. Often you'll also have to use a **model** to explain your theory or predict what might happen in the future. A model is just a mental picture of what's going on.

Theories are not fixed – they're a bit like clothes, you can change them when you like. The only difference is that you need new information and a good reason to change a theory.

Television investigator Miss Marple.

Some pieces of evidence give us more information than others.

Curiosity...created a new theory

A scientific theory can be created in many ways. Below is just one way it may be developed.

Investigations and experiments

⬇

Observations and results (data)

⬇

Inferences (mini-conclusions about different parts of the experiment)

⬇

Conclusions (which explain the observations and all the inferences)

⬇

Further investigations and experiments

⬇

Further observations and results (data)

⬇

Further inferences

⬇

Further conclusions

⬇

Alter or confirm the theory

The investigation might involve making a prediction that you test in the investigation

The results might come from measuring something or recording some information.

Your theory might lead you to test it in a further investigation, which will develop the theory.

The new results may make you change or question your original conclusion and alter your theory.

The theory about particles

Any theory or <u>model</u> of solids, liquids and gases must be able to explain what we see. See if the picture you have in your head of solids, liquids and gases matches the students' sketches.

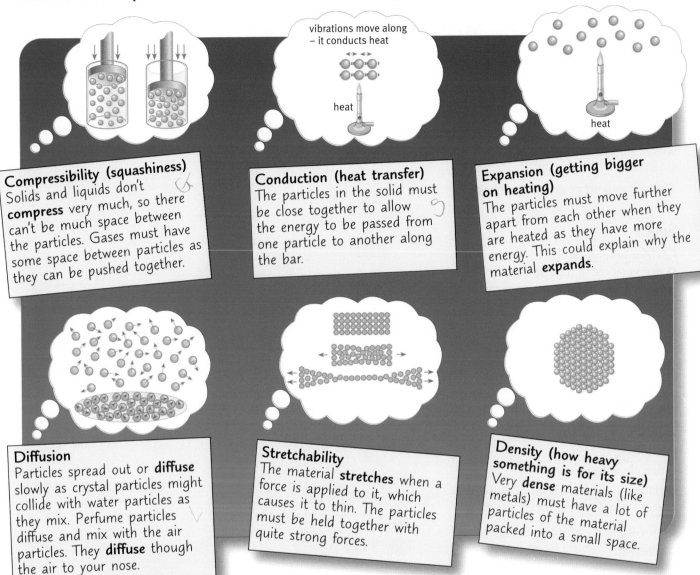

Compressibility (squashiness)
Solids and liquids don't **compress** very much, so there can't be much space between the particles. Gases must have some space between particles as they can be pushed together.

Conduction (heat transfer)
The particles in the solid must be close together to allow the energy to be passed from one particle to another along the bar.

Expansion (getting bigger on heating)
The particles must move further apart from each other when they are heated as they have more energy. This could explain why the material **expands**.

Diffusion
Particles spread out or **diffuse** slowly as crystal particles might collide with water particles as they mix. Perfume particles diffuse and mix with the air particles. They **diffuse** though the air to your nose.

Stretchability
The material **stretches** when a force is applied to it, which causes it to thin. The particles must be held together with quite strong forces.

Density (how heavy something is for its size)
Very **dense** materials (like metals) must have a lot of particles of the material packed into a small space.

Conclusion

Matter (material) is made up of tiny bits called **particles**. The arrangement of the particles, the space between them and the energy they have, gives us the three states of matter: solid, liquid and gas.

1 Copy and complete using words from the Language bank: A prediction is a _____ about something that can be tested by doing an _____.

2 Put the following in the order they normally occur: results, observations, inferences, conclusions, investigation aim, method.

Language bank

compress	investigation
conclusion	observation
conduct	particle
density	results
diffusion	stretch
expansion	theory
experiment	

○ How can the particle model explain the differences between solids, liquids and gases?

When we picture particles, it's as though we have a very powerful microscope and can see deep inside the material.
The particle theory takes all the experimental evidence we have about solids, liquids and gases and tries to explain them.

The three states of matter

Solids
Particles...
○ are very close together
○ have a small amount of energy
○ vibrate.

Liquids
Particles...
○ are close together
○ have a larger amount of energy than those in a solid
○ vibrate, but can also change places.

Gases
Particles...
○ are quite far apart (relative to their size)
○ have a large amount of energy
○ move rapidly in all directions.

The conclusions on the next page come from the experimental observations and inferences made on the last few pages. We use a model of particles to try to explain what we see.

Conclusion

Compressibility	Particles are very close together in solids and liquids but in gases they are far apart.
Conductivity (thermal)	The particles in a solid are very close together which allows energy to be transferred along the bar. In liquids and gases particles are further apart.
Expansion	As the particles have more energy, they vibrate more and move apart so the material gets bigger. The particles themselves do not expand.
Diffusion	Liquid and gas particles can spread out and mix. Gas particles move more quickly and so mix faster.
Stretchability	The forces holding the particles together in a solid are strong, but these are weaker in a liquid.
Density	The particles in dense materials must be very close together.

Detailed model to illustrate

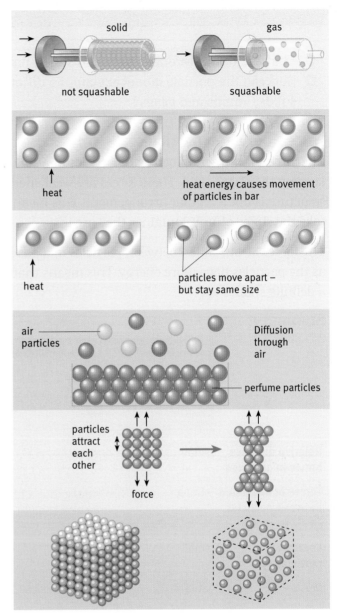

1 Copy and complete using words from the Language bank: The three _____ of matter are solid, _____ and gas. In solids and _____ the particles are very close together but in _____ they are far apart. The amount of energy the particles have is also different in solids, liquids and gases.

2 The air in a bike pump can be squashed. Why is it more difficult to squash a lump of iron?

3 Why do things expand when heated?

4 Do you think jelly is a solid, a liquid, or a gas?

Language bank

compressibility	model
conduct	particle
density	particle theory
diffusion	solid
expansion	states of matter
gases	stretch
liquid	theory
liquids	vibrate

○ What are the differences between solids liquids and gases?
○ How can the particle model explain the differences between solids, liquids and gases?

Forces between particles

The forces of attraction between particles in a solid are very strong, keeping the shape rigid. These forces are weakened in a liquid, so the structure is not a regular arrangement. This means that liquids can take the shape of any container they are in.

The forces of attraction between particles in a gas have been overcome as the particles have more energy. This means that a gas does not have a definite shape.

Summary

	Solid	Liquid	Gas
Relative distance between particles	small	small	large
Forces of attraction between particles	strong	strong (but a bit weaker than in solids)	no forces of attraction
Energy of particles	small	medium	large
Motion	vibrate	vibrate	move about

Tricky examples

Most substances are easy to classify as solid, a liquid or a gas. For example, iron is a solid, water is a liquid and oxygen is a gas. All you need to do is observe the material's shape, density, compressibility, and so on, and you'll be able to decide what its state of matter is. However, there are some substances that are a bit more difficult to classify.

Are these solid, liquids or gases?

Solids are rigid, but is paper? Liquids are less dense than solids but mercury is very dense...

We might also get runny solids or thick liquids. To classify everything as one of the three states of matter – solid, liquid or gas – can be difficult.

Guess what?
Nitrogen is a gas at normal room temperatures but if it's cooled below −196 °C it becomes a liquid. If you dipped soft things into it, they would take on new properties.

A daffodil dipped in liquid nitrogen becomes hard and brittle, and can be easily shattered by a hammer.

So is there air between the particles?

No, just gaps.

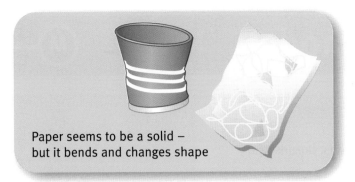

Paper seems to be a solid – but it bends and changes shape

Glass looks solid but its structure is more like a liquid's

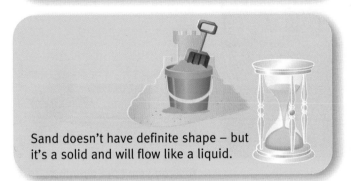

Sand doesn't have definite shape – but it's a solid and will flow like a liquid.

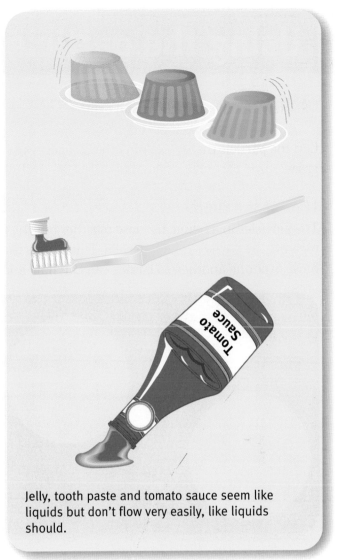

Jelly, tooth paste and tomato sauce seem like liquids but don't flow very easily, like liquids should.

1 Copy and complete using words from the Language bank: The particle model can be used to explain many of the things we see. The _____ _____ _____ between particles in a solid must be stronger than in a liquid and a gas. Many of the differences between solids, liquids and gases can be explained by distances between particles and the _____ (motion) of the particles.

2 Why is it easy to squash a gas but hard to squash a solid?

3 If a gas is hot its particles move around faster. Explain this in your own words.

4 Parminder suggests that her class act out the three states of matter for the rest of the year using themselves as particles. How do you think they should do this?

Language bank

energy
forces of attraction
gas
liquid
particle
solid
vibration

Using the particle model

○ How can the particle model explain other phenomena?

Can the particle theory explain other properties of solids, liquids and gases?

Liquids are runny

The particles in a liquid are close together but the forces holding them together are weaker than in a solid. This means that the particles can move over one another, so liquids can can flow and form puddles.

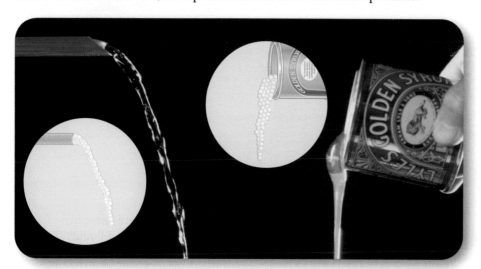

The particle model helps us to show what is happening when liquids are poured.

You can smell the tomato soup from across the room because of diffusion.

Solids and liquids have a definite volume – gases don't

There are no forces holding particles in gases together so they can spread out or diffuse and fill whatever space is available.

Diffusion tries to even out the spread of particles. Things tend to move from where there are lots of particles to where there aren't many.

Solids have a definite shape but liquids and gases do not

The forces that hold the particles together in a solid are quite strong. Those in a liquid are weaker and those in a gas are virtually non-existent. This means that solids are held in a rigid, definite shape, while liquids and gases take the shape of the container they are in.

Liquids can take any shape.

Dust particles seem to spread out in a beam of light

What makes the particles of dust in the beam of light seem to move? The dust reflects the light and can be seen moving around or diffusing, just like a bad smell moves around a room. The air particles are bumping into the dust, so diffusion is slow in air.

Coloured crystal particles in agar spread out slowly

The coloured crystal particles spread out very slowly because the agar is a thick jelly and the particles are closer together than they are in, say, water. The coloured particles break off from the crystal and bump into more particles in the agar than they would in water, so diffusion is slow.

Crystal particles diffuse more quickly in water than they do in agar.

Particles of dust, reflected in a beam of light, can be seen diffusing through the air.

Changing state

In **changing state** from a solid to a liquid to a gas, the particles themselves don't change. The things that change are:

o the distance between particles;

o the energy of the particles (how quickly they move).

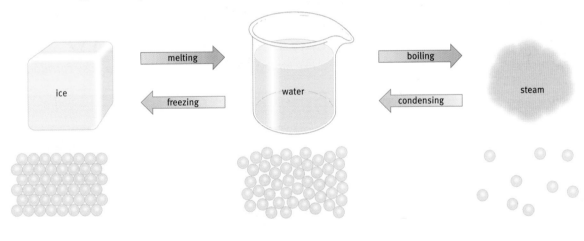

1 Copy and complete using words from the Language bank: All matter is made up of tiny particles. When matter changes from a solid to a liquid to a _____, the distance between the particles, and how quickly they move, change.

2 Why do the purple crystals take a long time to spread out in the agar jelly?

3 Name the following changes in state:

   a gas to liquid   **b** solid to liquid   **c** liquid to gas   **d** liquid to solid
   e solid to gas

4 Why do liquids form puddles but solids don't?

Language bank

agar
boiling
condensing
freezing
gas
liquid
melting
particle model
solid

○ **How can the particle model explain other phenomena?**

The particle model can be used to explain things we can see and things we don't see.

Diffusion

Like hot water gives of steam, liquid bromine gives off bromine vapour. This **diffuses** slowly through air. But when bromine diffuses into a vacuum, it does so in less than a second.

Using the particle theory, we can suggest a reason.

The downside of diffusion...

In air *The bromine particles try to spread out, but bump into air particles that are already there. This makes the diffusion process slow...*

...like Mr Bromine trying to walk down a busy corridor.

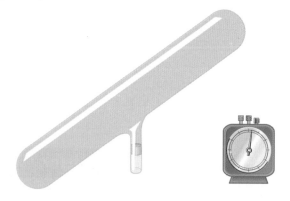

In a vacuum *Diffusion happens almost instantly and the coloured particles fill the container very quickly. This happens because there is no air in the way as the bromine particles move about. They diffuse much more quickly in a vacuum than in air...*

...like Mr Bromine walking down an empty corridor.

Gases exert a pressure

Gas particles move round at incredible speeds in every direction. They **collide** with (bump into) each other and the sides of the container they are in. This is what causes gas pressure.

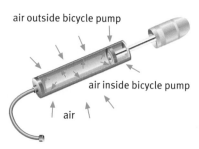

Gas pressure is caused by colliding gas particles.

Why can a can collapse?

Apparatus
Empty can, tripod, Bunsen burner.

Method
1 Place a small amount of water in a can.
2 Heat the can and water with a Bunsen burner until the water boils.
3 After a few minutes remove the heat and place the lid on the can.
4 Note down your observations.

Results
When the can cools down the steam cools and condenses, making the pressure inside the can less than outside. As a result the can collapses.

Analysis
The particle theory can be used to explain what we see and what we don't see.

Conclusion
In the diagrams shown on the right, the arrows represent a collision between an air particle and the can. Normally the air particles hit the can on the outside and the inside equally. But when there are more air particles hitting the outside of the can than the inside, the can collapses. The same effect can be seen by connecting the can to a vacuum pump that removes the air particles. The vacuum pump does not suck the can inwards. It's the air particles hitting the outside of the can that do the pushing and squash the can.

You can't see air pressure, only the effect of it – in this case, the crushed can.

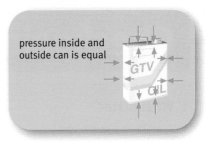

Before...

...during...

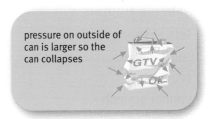

...and after.

1 Gas _____ are moving around all the time. Gas _____ is caused by particles hitting the walls of the container they are in.

2 Why can perfume and aftershave be smelt across a room?

3 If a tube of hydrogen gas is placed above a test tube of air, why would the tube of air give a positive test for hydrogen (the squeaky pop test) after a few minutes?

4 Summarise the particle theory in a poster.

Language bank ○

bromine
collapse
collide
diffuse
particle theory
particles
pressure
vacuum

Checkpoint

1 What state?

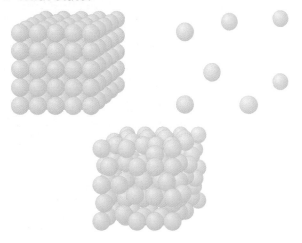

Look at the particle diagrams. Copy them, using a different colour for each and leaving plenty of space around them. Write the following labels round the correct diagram. Put a heading for each diagram showing which state it represents.

lots of space

touching

touching

cannot squash

can squash

cannot squash

do not conduct heat

conduct heat well

conduct heat poorly

moving fast in all directions

regularly arranged

randomly arranged

2 True or false?

Decide whether the following statements are true or false. Write down the true ones. Correct the false ones before you write them down.

a Solids expand when you heat them because the particles get bigger.

b In a gas the particles are moving fast in all directions, with no forces of attraction between them.

c In a liquid there are very strong forces of attraction between the particles.

d The forces of attraction between the particles are strongest in a solid.

3 Moving around

Copy and complete these sentences, unscrambling the words.

o The particles in **squidli** and gases can move around.

o Because of this, they can spread and mix. We call this **suffinoid**.

o The particles in gases shoot around and hit each other. They also hit the walls of their **nitancor**, exerting **sag serrupre**.

4 Choose the answer

Copy and complete these sentences, choosing the correct ending.

You heat a solid. The particles are given enough energy to break the strong forces of attraction between them, and they can move around. The solid has

evaporated

melted

diffused

expanded

5 Mind map

Draw a mind map for this topic using the following words. Add more words where you want.

Particle model of matter

solids*

liquids*

gases*

melting

freezing

condensing

evaporating

* add descriptions of how the particles behave

Solutions

Before starting this unit, you should already be familiar with these ideas from earlier work.

- You can dissolve some (but not all) solids in water. If you dissolve salt in water, what is the name of the clear mixture of salt and water?
- Dissolving is not the same as melting. Can you explain the difference?
- If you have an insoluble solid, such as sand, mixed with water, you can separate the mixture quite easily. What method do you use?
- You can separate a solution by heating it to evaporate the liquid, then condensing the liquid again. What is the name of this process?
- Solids, liquids and gases are made up of particles. How do the particles move differently in solids and liquids?

You will meet these key ideas as you work through this unit. Have a quick look now, and at the end of the unit read through them slowly.

- When a solid dissolves to form a solution, the mass does not change. For example, if you dissolve 50 g of salt in 100 g of water, the solution will have a mass of 150 g. We say that **mass is conserved**.
- Mass is conserved because the salt and water particles are all still there when you make a solution. You have not lost any matter – you still have all the salt and water that you started with.
- When a solid dissolves, the particles in the liquid bump into the solid particles and surround them. Individual solid particles get carried off the surface of the solid and intermingle with the liquid particles.
- You can speed up dissolving if you heat the mixture.
- If you keep adding more solid to a solution, eventually no more will dissolve. Some solid will be left in the bottom. The solution is now **saturated**.
- A solution is saturated when the liquid particles cannot surround and carry away any more solid particles.

Pure or mixture?

○ How can we tell whether a liquid is mixture?
○ How much salt can we get from rock salt?

A **pure** substance contains only *one* substance. Pure water is made up of just water. A substance is a **mixture** if it can be separated into other substances.

Most things we use are not pure – they're mixtures. Some mixtures are easy to spot, like cough mixture. Tap water looks pure, but is in fact water mixed with fine particles of silt, and chemicals to keep it clean.

Mixtures are separated using simple **separation techniques** (a technique is just a way of doing something).

Solutes, solvents and solutions

If a solid dissolves in water we call it a **soluble** solid. If the solid doesn't dissolve, then it is called an **insoluble** solid.

The liquid doing the dissolving is called the **solvent** and the substance being dissolved is called the **solute**. When they mix they form a **solution**.

solute + solvent → solution

sugar + water → sugary water

Rock salt

Salt is found in sea water and in rock salt. Rock salt is really a mixture of salt and bits of rock. Because the salt is soluble in water and the rock isn't, the two can be separated in three steps:

The sea is a mixture of water, salt and many other bits and pieces. Some of these you can see quite easily (like the fish and boats) and others you can't (like the salt). This means some bits are easier to separate than others.

A salt mine under Cheshire.

1 Dissolving – which adds water, dissolving the salt.

2 Filtering – which removes the bits of rock.

3a Evaporating to dryness – which removes the water from the salt.

glass rod

rock salt

The salt dissolves because it's soluble. The rock doesn't as it's insoluble.

The large lumps of undissolved rock can't fit through the holes in the filter paper, but the salty water can.

The water boils off and leaves the dissolved salt behind.

3b Alternatively, the salty water could be distilled.

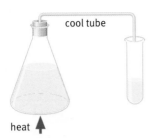

The liquid boils off and then is cooled, condensed and collected. This is good for collecting the solvent but not for getting the solute.

Brine lakes or evaporation ponds are sometimes used to separate the salt from water.

Interesting facts about salt

Common salt is sodium chloride, a compound of sodium and chloride.

Salt tax was one of the causes of the French Revolution.

There are 4.5 million cubic miles of salt in the sea.

Salt was once used for cleaning teeth

Salt is used to flavour food.

Salt is put on roads to prevent ice from forming.

Medieval babies were rubbed in salt to bring good luck.

Salt is used to make chlorine gas. This gas is then used to make plastics and bleach.

Salt is used to make sodium hydroxide (an important alkali).

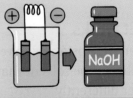

1 Copy and complete using words from the Language bank: Rock salt is a _____ of salt and rock. Pure salt can be made using the _____ techniques of dissolving, _____, _____ or _____.

2 Why would the amount of salt obtained from rock salt be less than the mass you started with?

3 What is salt used for? Write a short report describing its uses. Are there any hazards associated with using salt?

4 The word 'salary' means 'wage' and comes from the Latin word *salarium*. Find out what a *salarium* was and how it is linked to the word 'salary'.

Language bank ○━

dissolving
distilling
evaporating
filtering
insoluble
mixture
rock salt
separation techniques
soluble
solute
solution
solvent

Chromatography

○ **How can chromatography identify and separate substances in mixtures?**

You may have used **chromatography** to **separate** dyes in inks in primary school. But chromatography is not just used for separating inks. Hospitals use chromatography in chemical analysis to separate and examine blood. So do **forensic scientists** working with the police to help solve crimes.

A forensic team at the scene of a crime.

What does chromatography separate?

A mixture of two or more **solutes** that are **soluble** in a certain **solvent** can be separated by chromatography. For example, the different coloured dyes in a Smartie or the green pigments in leaves can be separated.

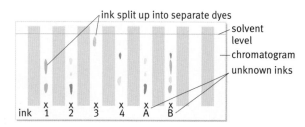

A chromatogram of four known inks. Unknown ink A is ink 2, and unknown in B is a mixture of inks 1 and 4.

How it works

○ Different substances have different **solubilities**, so one will be more soluble in the solvent than another – and substances will stick to the paper differently.

○ As the solvent washes through the paper, it carries the ink with it. The solutes in the ink that are more soluble and stick to the paper less will be carried further up the paper than those that are less soluble and stick to the paper more. This separates them into bands of colour. The 'picture' this creates is called a **chromatogram**.

The chemicals being separated are not always coloured. Scientists may use a stain or ultraviolet light to see the patches of different substances.

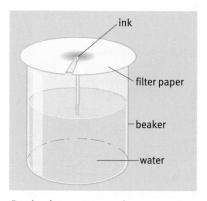

Basic chromatography apparatus.

Picture it like this: Imagine the river as the solvent washing the different teams (substances) down the river. The people hold on to the rocks (the paper) differently, so are washed (separated) to different places.

Using chromatography

Forensic science is the use of science and technology to gather evidence and solve crimes. Chromatography is used in forensic science to do things like examine urine and blood for traces of alcohol or drugs. A paint sample can also be analysed using chromatography to find out about the car it came from. Scientists can work out not only the model of the car, but also the year it was made!

Water quality, air pollution and the nutritional content of food can also be determined by chromatography.

Weightlifter Ashot Danielyan was stripped of his bronze medal when he tested positive for the steroid stanozolol at the 2000 Sydney Olympic Games.

Chromatography is used to examine blood.

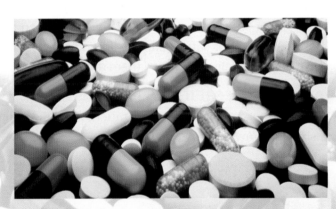

Many medical drugs and chemicals have to be produced in a pure form. Chromatography is used to analyse and monitor their quality and level of purity.

Language bank

analyse
chromatogram
chromatography
dissolved
forensic science
monitor
purity
solute
soluble
solvent

1 Copy and complete using words from the Language bank:
   _____ can be used to separate a mixture of two or more solutes that are _____ in a particular solvent. It can be used to separate chemicals or different colours in inks and dyes and is important in _____ science.

2 What is forensic science?

3 Chromatography has become so sensitive that it can separate and identify different samples of blood. Why might this be useful?

O **Is there a limit to the amount of solid that will dissolve in a liquid?**

O **What else affects solubility?**

Solubility tells us how much of something can dissolve in something else. You will know from making tea that things dissolve better if:

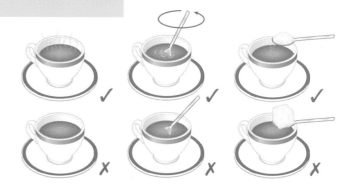

O the liquid is hot: the hotter the liquid the faster something dissolves;

O you stir the liquid: the quicker you stir the faster something dissolves;

O you have small bits of solid to dissolve: the smaller the bits the faster something dissolves.

When a solid dissolves, the particles in the liquid bump into the solid particles and surround them. The solid particles are carried off and intermingle with the liquid.

You probably know that there's a limit to how much sugar you can dissolve. That's because the liquid will not **hold** any more of the sugar – so the sugar sinks to the bottom of the cup. When this happens, we say that the solution is **saturated**. The liquid particles cannot surround any more solid particles and carry them away.

A saturated solution of salt.

Investigating saturated solutions

A simple method for seeing how much of a solid will dissolve in a liquid is shown below.

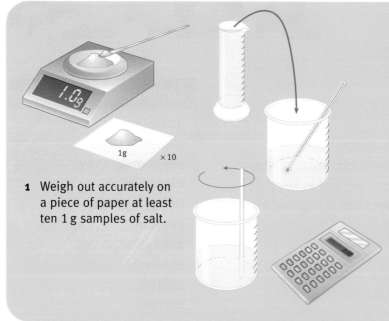

1 Weigh out accurately on a piece of paper at least ten 1 g samples of salt.

2 Measure out 25 cm³ of water using a measuring cylinder. Note down the temperature of the water.

3 Put one of the 1 g samples of salt into the water and stir it round ten times using using a glass rod and measure the temperature.

4 Continue adding 1 g at a time, noting how much you've added, until no more salt will dissolve. The amount that will dissolve will be 1g less than the figure you finish with.

5 Solubility is measured in grams per 100 g of water. 100 cm³ of water = 100 g. So the figure you discovered needs to be multiplied by 4 to give the units g/100 g (because you used only 25 cm³ of water).

More about solubilities

Different solids have different solubilities and solutes are more soluble at higher temperatures

These differences can be represented on a graph:

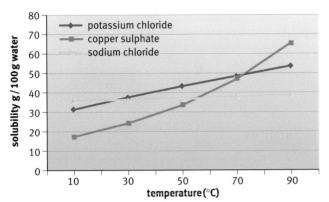

Typical solubility curves.

At a certain temperature some solids are more soluble than others: for example, the solid potassium chloride is more soluble than the solids potassium bromide and potassium iodide.

At 30 °C, 37.6 g of potassium chloride will dissolve in 100 g water. Only 24.2 g of copper sulphate will dissolve in the same amount of water.

The higher the temperature, the more soluble the solid becomes. This is because the particles have more energy and move around more quickly. The faster liquid particles bump into the solid particles more often and carry them away faster.

For this reason, you should always state the temperature when you say how soluble something is. For example: 'Potassium chloride has a solubility of 37.6 g/100 g of water at 30 °C.'

Solubility of solids changes in different solvents

Solvents only dissolve certain substances. For example, solid nail varnish won't dissolve in water, but it will dissolve in nail varnish remover (propanone).

1 Copy and complete using words from the Language bank. When a soluble substance is added to a liquid, eventually no more will _____. Every substance has its own _____ so a certain solvent will dissolve different amounts of substances. Most solutes become more soluble as their _____ is increased.

2 The data below shows how the solubility of a certain substance (solid X) changes with temperature.

 a Draw a line graph of solubility (*y* axis) versus temperature (*x* axis).

 b Use your graph to find how much solid X could be dissolved at 30 °C and at 90 °C in 100 g of water.

Solubility (g/100g water)	Temperature (°C)
13	0
21	10
32	20
64	40
110	60
169	80

3 Water is not the only solvent. Find out the names of two other solvents.

Guess what?

Dry cleaning isn't really dry. A range of liquid solvents is used to remove stains, but not usually water. The smell at the dry cleaners is evaporated solvent.

Language bank

dissolve
potassium chloride
propanone
saturated solution
solubility
temperature

○ **What happens to the solute when a solution is made?**
○ **How can we separate solvents from solutes?**

Many words that we use in science have other meanings outside science. For example, in science the word 'solution' is used to mean something that contains a solute dissolved in a solvent.

Coffee is a solution.

Inside solutions

When 5 g of rice are mixed with 10 g of dried peas, unsurprisingly we get a 15 g mixture of rice and peas.

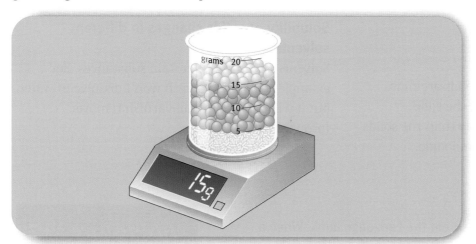

Is dissolving disappearing?

No. When 5 g of salt dissolves in 10 g of water, the solid doesn't disappear. We know this because the solution of salt water has a mass of 15 g.

The particles of salt and the particles of water intermingle (mix up). Even though you can't see the salt, it's still there. Nothing is lost.

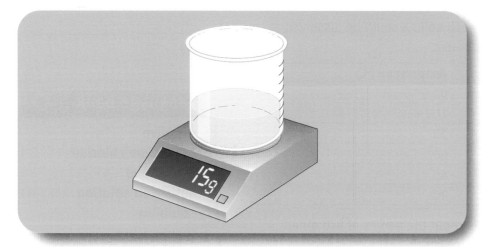

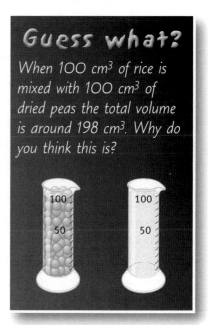

Guess what?

When 100 cm³ of rice is mixed with 100 cm³ of dried peas the total volume is around 198 cm³. Why do you think this is?

So is dissolving the same as melting?

No, dissolving is when solid particles mix with liquid particles. Melting is a solid turning into a liquid.

The particles remain unchanged as they mix together.

Separating a solvent from solutes

To separate and collect a solvent from a solute, or one solvent from another, distillation is the best method to use. For example, pure water can be distilled from sea water.

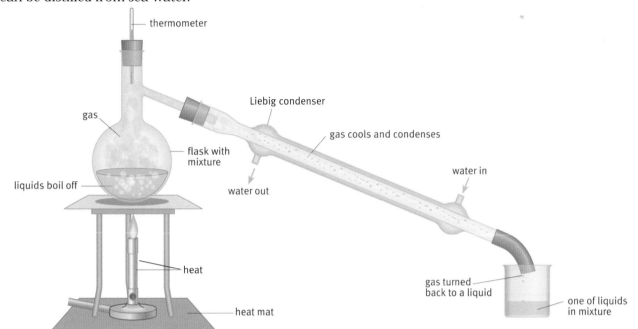

Distillation involves boiling, condensing and collecting:
1 The liquid is heated so it boils off and turns into a gas.
2 The gas is then cooled in the condenser so turns back into a liquid.
3 The liquid then runs down the condenser to the beaker, where it's collected.
4 The solute stays in the flask you heated it in, and does not boil off.

Salt is removed from sea water at large desalination plants.

1 Copy and complete using words from the Language bank: When a solute dissolves, the solute and solvent particles _____.
Distillation can be used to separate a _____ from the _____ that are dissolved in it. Distillation involves _____ a liquid so it turns into a gas, and then _____ it so that it becomes a liquid again.

2 Explain the meaning of the following words:
   a solution
   b saturate

3 Water will evaporate into a gas at any temperature. The gas cools on cold surfaces to become water again. How could people on a desert island obtain pure water from sea water using a large plastic sheet and a bucket?

4 Draw a flow chart to explain all the different processes involved when drinking water is made from sea water using the distillation apparatus above.

Language bank

boiling
condensation
condensing
dissolve
distillation
evaporation
intermingle
solutes
solution
solvent

Checkpoint

1 Words beginning with 's'

Match up the beginnings and endings to make complete sentences. Use a different colour to write each sentence.

Beginnings

A solution is

A solid that is dissolved in a liquid is called a

A liquid with solid dissolved in it is called a

A saturated solution is

Endings

a solution in which no more solute will dissolve.

a mixture of a solvent and a solute.

solvent.

solute.

2 It's your choice

Copy and complete the following sentences. Choose the correct ending.

If you dissolve 5 g of salt in 100 g of water, you will have a solution with a mass of **95 g / 150 g / 105 g**

This shows the **conservation of mass / conservationist's theory of mass / conversation model**

You still have the same number of salt and water **beakers / particles / cells**

3 Which kit?

Choose a set of apparatus from the kit list to separate each mixture. Write short notes or make a labelled sketch to show how you would separate each one.

Mixtures

sand in water

different coloured inks in a felt-tip pen

sugar from a sugar solution

Kit list

flask, condenser, Bunsen burner, beaker

flask, filter funnel, filter paper

chromatography paper, solvent, tank

4 True or false?

Decide whether the following statements are true or false. Write down the true ones. Correct the false ones before you write them down.

a The amount of a solid that will dissolve at a certain temperature is the solubility.

b Solubility does not change with temperature.

c Different solids all have the same solubility.

d Solubility is measured in grams per 100 g of solvent.

5 When things dissolve

Match up the beginnings and endings to make complete sentences. Use a different colour to write each sentence.

Beginnings

Before you make a solution, the particles in the solid are

When you mix the solid and liquid, the particles in the liquid

When the solid dissolves,

When the solution is saturated,

Endings

the solvent particles surround the solute particles.

fixed in position and vibrating.

the solvent cannot hold any more solute particles.

move around and collide with the solid.

Energy resources

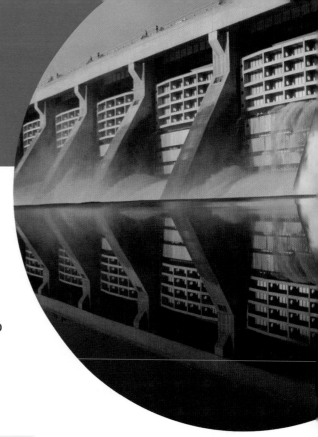

Before starting this unit, you should already be familiar with these ideas from earlier work.

○ When you burn something, new materials are made. What else happens when something burns? Think about what you see, feel and hear.

○ Plants make their own food so that they can grow. What process do they use to make their food, and what do they need for it?

○ Animals need food for growth. Where do animals get their food?

You will meet these key ideas as you work through this unit. Have a quick look now, and at the end of the unit read through them slowly.

○ We use a range of **fuels** to make things happen. Fuels include gas, coal, wood, and many other substances which we burn. Food is the fuel for our bodies.

○ When fuels make things happen, they are releasing **energy**.

○ A non-living system such as a car burns fuel to provide energy so it can move. A living system such as a human uses the fuel from its food to provide energy for all its life processes.

○ Fuels are vital to us because they provide us with energy to do many things, such as heat our homes, cook, and also make things and move things. We use a lot of fuel to generate electricity.

○ Coal, oil and natural gas are **fossil fuels**. Fossil fuels took millions of years to form, and we are using them up quickly. We need to **conserve** fuels by reducing the amount of energy we use.

○ We can also conserve fuels by using **renewable energy** resources. Some fuels can be replaced, such as wood. We can use other renewable resources such as wind turbines to generate electricity.

○ Energy can be **transferred** from one form to another. For example, in a hairdryer, electrical energy is transferred to heat energy, movement energy and sound energy.

○ Living things also transfer energy. Plants transfer light energy from the Sun to chemical energy when they photosynthesise. Animals eat plants. They transfer the chemical energy in their food into other forms of energy such as movement, sound, and heat.

Why are fuels useful?

A **fuel** is a substance that releases **energy** when it burns. Which of these fuels do you use at home and school? What are they used for?

Common fuels: coal, natural gas, and paraffin.

The Bunsen burner

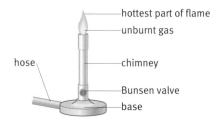

- hottest part of flame
- unburnt gas
- chimney
- Bunsen valve
- base
- hose

The Bunsen burner burns natural gas (mainly methane). The valve controls how much air mixes with the gas before it burns. This adjusts the flame temperature.

Heating substances — safely

How to light a Bunsen

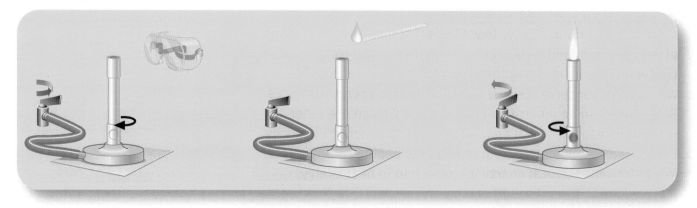

1 Put on goggles and place the Bunsen on a heat-proof mat.

2 Close the Bunsen's valve.

3 Turn the gas tap to half open.

4 Light the Bunsen with a lighted splint. (Light your splint from your teacher's Bunsen.)

5 If told to, open the tap fully to increase the size of the flame.

6 The valve can be opened to change the flame colour and temperature.

7 When the burner is not in use, turn the valve to give a yellow flame and remove it from underneath the apparatus.

> Used properly the Bunsen burner is a safe piece of apparatus. Used incorrectly it's dangerous and could harm you, or your friends.

✓ Do
- ✓ Light it properly
- ✓ Turn it to yellow flame when not in use
- ✓ Use a heat-proof mat
- ✓ Use a splint
- ✓ Wear goggles when heating

✗ Don't
- ✗ Light it with the valve open
- ✗ Use a match to light it
- ✗ Burn things in it unless told to do so

Investigating the Bunsen flame

The valve of the Bunsen can be opened or closed (or positioned somewhere in between) depending on what you're heating. The properties of the flame when the valve is in different positions are shown below.

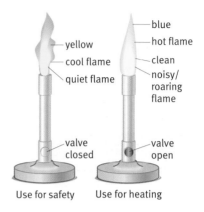

blue
hot flame
yellow
cool flame
clean
quiet flame
noisy/roaring flame
valve closed
valve open

Use for safety   Use for heating

Valve	Flame	Noise	Used for
closed	yellow sooty	quiet flame	safety
open	blue hot clean	noisy/roaring flame	heating

Heating apparatus

You will use apparatus similar to this to heat materials:

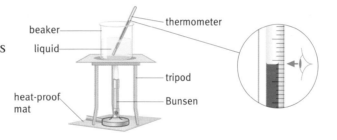

thermometer
beaker
liquid
tripod
heat-proof mat
Bunsen

Thermometers

Temperature is measured using a thermometer. When reading the scale on a thermometer make sure your eye is level with the scale. The level of the alcohol in a thermometer may curve so take your reading from the bottom of the curve. The curve is called the **meniscus**.

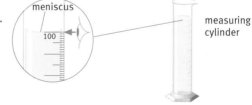

meniscus
100
measuring cylinder

1. Copy and complete using words from the Language bank: Fuels are substances that burn to release _____. Examples of fuels include coal, and _____ gas. The _____ burner is used to heat substances. It burns the gas _____ to produce a flame. When the _____ is open, the flame burns blue.

2. Describe in your own words how to light a Bunsen burner safely.

3. List the apparatus you would need to heat 25 cm³ of water to 65 °C safely.

Language bank

alcohol
Bunsen burner
Celsius (°C)
energy
fuel
meniscus
methane (natural gas)
thermometer
valve

○ What are fossil fuels?

Coal, oil and natural gas are called **fossil fuels** because they formed over 300 million years ago from the remains of **organic** material like dead plants and animals. They store **chemical energy** which they release as other forms of energy like heat and light when they're burnt. For this reason they're known as **energy resources**.

Many fossil fuels come from crude oil.

Common fossil fuels or energy resources

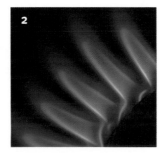

1 Coal
used for domestic heating and industrially for generating electricity

2 Natural gas (mainly methane)
used domestically (in homes) for heating and cooking and industrially to generate electricity

3 Butane and propane
used domestically in heating and LPG fuels and industrially in ships

4 Petrol and diesel (from oil)
used domestically as a fuel for cars, boats and chain-saws and industrially as a fuel for lorries and vans

5 Paraffin (kerosene)
used domestically in heating things like greenhouses and industrially as an aviation fuel

Where do fossil fuels come from?

Ancient plants used the Sun's energy to live and grow. It's this energy that's being released when we burn fossil fuels.

Oil and natural gas

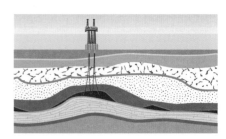

1 Tiny sea creatures died and sank to the sea floor.

2 They were covered in layers of sand and mud which turned to rock over millions of years. Heat and pressure inside the Earth eventually turned their remains to liquid oil and gas.

3 The gas and oil were squeezed through tiny holes in rocks until they reached a rock layer they couldn't pass through. Gas and oil deposits collected.

Coal

1 Trees died and fell into swamps, forming layers of swampy material.

2 The layers were covered by mud and sand.

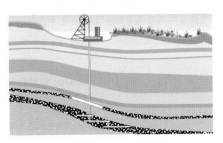

3 The layers were pressurised and heated over millions of years and turned into layers of hard coal.

Because they take so long to form, fossil fuels are known as **non-renewable** resources. This means that we cannot replace them and one day they'll run out.

The advantages and disadvantages of fuels

The amount of energy a fuel gives out is important, but is it the only thing you should consider? Are there cases where a gas is better than a liquid?

Fuel	Fossil fuel?	State	Energy released per 1 g of fuel (kJ)
wood	✘	solid	10
coal	✔	solid	27
natural gas	✔	gas	40
charcoal	✘	solid	34
oil	✔	liquid	46
coke	✔	solid	30
butane	✔	gas	49
propane	✔	gas	50

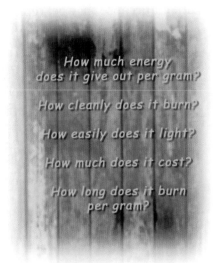

How much energy does it give out per gram?

How cleanly does it burn?

How easily does it light?

How much does it cost?

How long does it burn per gram?

Some questions you might ask about fuels.

Some fuels are better than others for a certain job. For example, you might find that petrol is more convenient to use in a car's engine than coal...but you can use gas like liquefied petroleum gas (LPG) to run a car.

1 Copy and complete using words from the Language bank: Coal, mineral oil and natural _____ are examples of _____ fuels, which have been formed from _____ material like dead plants and animals over many millions of years. These fuels are _____, which means that we cannot replace them and they will eventually run out.

2 Why are these fuels known as fossil fuels?

3 Name six examples of fossil fuels.

4 Wood gives out relatively little energy when burnt. Why do you think it is used so much in some countries, like Norway?

5 Which fuel would you use on a barbecue? Why is this fuel better than, say, oil?

6 Why is LPG becoming popular as an alternative fuel for cars?

Language bank

butane
chemical energy
coal
diesel
energy resource
fossil fuel
kerosene
Liquid Petroleum Gas (LPG)
natural gas
non-renewable resources
organic
paraffin
peat
petrol
propane

○ What are renewable energy resources?

As a nation we are using more energy resources every year. Fossil fuels are being made today, but unfortunately they take between 300 and 500 million years to form – that's a long time to wait for a bag of coal! Instead we must look towards **renewable** energy resources to meet our energy needs. Renewable energy resources are resources that will not run out because they get replaced.

A turbine and generator at a nuclear power station.

Generating electricity

Most of our electricity comes from power stations, where it is produced using huge machines called generators. Many large power stations burn coal, oil, or natural gas. The heat is used to boil water to make steam. The steam turns turbines which drive the generators.

The energy in the fuel originally came from the Sun. The power station changes this into electrical energy:

Sun's energy → stored energy in fuel → heat → movement energy → electrical energy

In some large power stations, the heat comes from a nuclear reactor.

Types of renewable energy used to generate electricity

There are several renewable energy resources currently available. Others are being investigated all the time.

(Active) solar panels
Energy from the Sun is used to heat up water that can be used in the house.

Solar cells
Solar cells on the new type of cat's eye. The solar cell uses the Sun's light energy to produce an electric current.

Hydroelectric power (HEP)
Water runs down the pipe and turns the turbine. This is connected to a generator that produces electricity.

Wind power
Modern turbines on 'wind farms' work in the same way as traditional windmills. But the turbines are connected to generators rather than grindstones.

Wave power
The wave compresses air in a tube that drives a turbine and a generator. Other designs have large duck-shaped devices moving up and down with the movement of waves. This movement is used to generate electricity. This design is not often used.

Tidal power
Tidal power stations are usually built on estuaries where rivers flow into the sea. When the tide comes in, water moves past the turbines and is trapped. When the tide goes out, the opposite happens – water is released through the turbine in the other direction. Both movements generate electricity.

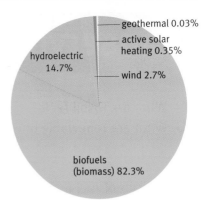

geothermal 0.03%
active solar heating 0.35%
hydroelectric 14.7%
wind 2.7%
biofuels (biomass) 82.3%

Some of our renewable energy resources. Around 2.8% of our electrical needs are met by renewable energy resources. This figure is due to rise over the next few years.

Geothermal power
The rocks below the Earth's surface are hot. This heat is used to make steam which drives turbines and generators. (This is not commonly used in the UK, but very popular in California, USA.)

Biofuel or biomass
Wood is a very common biofuel. Also, waste material and animal faeces can be used to make flammable gases like methane. This happens in sewage treatment plants and is sometimes called biogas.

1 Copy and complete using words from the Language bank: Renewable energy resources include wind, waves, running water (or _____ power), sunlight, biomass and some geothermal sources. Renewable energy resources are used to generate _____.

2 Why might someone describe electricity as the most useful form of energy?

3 Describe simply how a hydroelectric power station works.

4 Some scientists argue that HEP dams may silt up and hot rock may cool, so tidal and solar energy are the only ones that are renewable and will truly 'not run out'. Do you agree with this statement? Give reasons for your answer.

5 Why does 'renewable' not mean 'reusable?'

6 About 20 wind turbines can produce enough electricity for about 15,000 homes but some people think they're ugly. List the advantages and disadvantages of having a wind turbine near your home.

Language bank

active solar heating
biofuel
electricity
generator
geothermal power
hydroelectric power
methane
renewables
resources
solar power
tidal power
turbine
wave power
wind power

Conserving energy

Fuel conservation

The amount of fuel and energy each of us uses will determine how long the world's fuel stocks last. This is what **energy conservation** is all about – using the minimum.

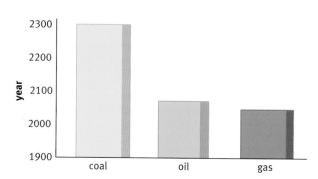

The bar chart opposite shows when we think the three main fossil fuels will run out. New reserves of gas and oil are still being discovered, but we aren't sure exactly how long supplies will last. What we do know is that these **non-renewable resources** will eventually run out, so conserving (saving) them is very important.

How to save energy

Saving energy does not have to be painful...you won't have to go to a school on a pogo stick...unless you fancy it...

Saving energy:
○ saves the world's resources, so they last longer
○ saves you money
○ reduces pollution

What can you do?
○ Turn lights off when you're not using them.
○ When making tea, boil only as much water in the kettle as you need. If everyone in the UK did this, one fossil fuel power station could be switched off.
○ Cycle instead of getting a lift, or share lifts with friends or neighbours. You and the environment will benefit.

What can you and your family do?
Putting your house in order:
○ Turn the heating down – it uses less fuel.
○ Buy low-energy light bulbs – they use less electricity.
○ Prevent draughts – heat is wasted through gaps around doors and windows.
○ Insulate your loft using glass fibre. Glass fibre has tiny pockets of air, which help to reduce heat loss.
○ Install double glazing – the air gap or vacuum between the two panes of glass prevents heat loss.
○ Lag the hot water tank – covering the tank in a special insulating

A low-energy light bulb.

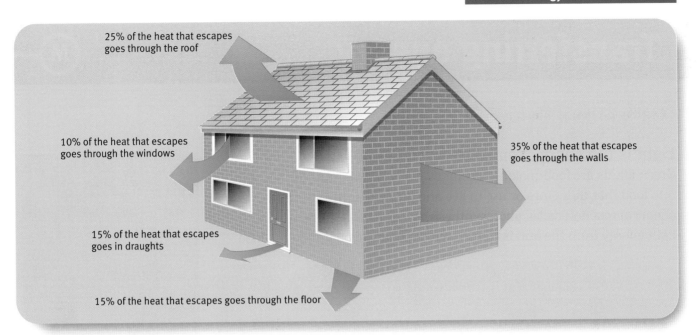

25% of the heat that escapes goes through the roof

10% of the heat that escapes goes through the windows

35% of the heat that escapes goes through the walls

15% of the heat that escapes goes in draughts

15% of the heat that escapes goes through the floor

Where does the heat go?

    jacket reduces heat loss.

What can we do as a nation?

o Don't use greedy gas-guzzling vehicles.

o Encourage pollution taxes, e.g. if you drive a car with a small engine, you pay less road tax.

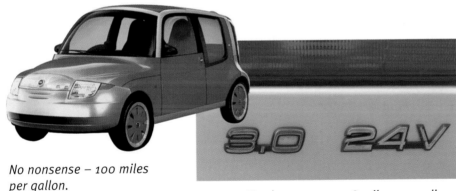

No nonsense – 100 miles per gallon.

Total nonsense – 18 miles per gallon.

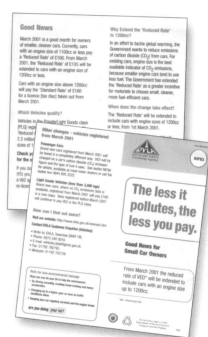

The less it pollutes, the less you pay.

A government leaflet designed to encourage people to drive smaller, cleaner cars.

1 Copy and complete using words from the Language bank:
  _____ energy resources will not run out, while _____ energy resources will eventually run out. Saving energy saves you money and saves the world's _____ , and reduces _____ .

2 Why is it important that we conserve our fuel resources?

3 List three ways that you and the environment would benefit if you cycled to school instead of getting a lift in a car.

4 Conduct a survey on how pupils in your class travel to school. Display your results in a bar chart. You could extend this to how teachers travel to school as well.

Language bank

conservation
conserving
insulation
lagging
non-renewable
renewable
pollution
resources

○ **How do living things use energy?**

Light is the energy source of green plants

Green plants are food-making machines. They convert simple chemicals into food that they store or use to live and grow. This involves a chemical reaction called **photosynthesis**, which needs sunlight. The light energy from the Sun is transferred to chemical energy in the food.

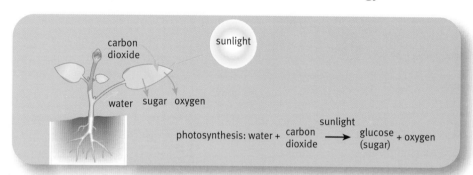

photosynthesis: water + carbon dioxide $\xrightarrow{\text{sunlight}}$ glucose (sugar) + oxygen

Plants change light energy into chemical energy.

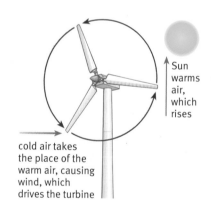

Guess what?

Not all the energy in the light becomes chemical energy. So where does it go? Some light energy turns into heat and warms the plant up, allowing other essential reactions to happen effectively.

The Sun is the most important energy source

The Sun is the source of almost all the Earth's energy resources. The ancient plants that formed coal millions of years ago transferred the Sun's light energy into chemical energy, just like plants do today. When we burn fuels we transfer this energy into heat and light.

light energy → chemical energy → heat + light energy
from the Sun   in plant material

The Sun even helps drive wind turbines. It is energy from the Sun that warms up the air, causing the winds that drive wind turbines.

Sun warms air, which rises

cold air takes the place of the warm air, causing wind, which drives the turbine

light energy → heat → movement energy → electrical energy

The Sun's warmth causes the winds that drive wind turbines.

Food is the energy source of animals

Animals might be intelligent organisms, but they can't transfer the Sun's energy into food like plants can. Animals need to eat plants and sometimes other animals (which have eaten plants) to gain enough energy to stay alive.

Food is the fuel that gives us energy and keeps us alive. The chemical reaction that changes food into energy that cells can use is called **respiration**.

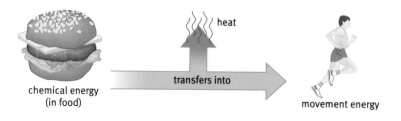

chemical energy (in food)   transfers into   heat   movement energy

How much energy does food contain?

If you burn a known mass of a certain food, like a crisp, you can use the heat to warm up some water. The more energy the crisp contains, the hotter the water becomes. Do you think all the heat gets to the water?

light energy → chemical energy → heat
in sunlight   in potato plant   in flame

Energy is measured in **joules** (J) but calories, the old unit, are still given on some food labels. A **kilojoule** is a thousand joules.

Energy transfers

Engines transfer one type of energy into another. Again, some energy is lost every time energy is transferred.

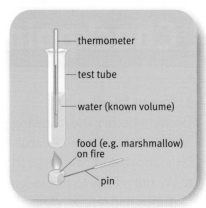

The energy the food releases heats up the water.

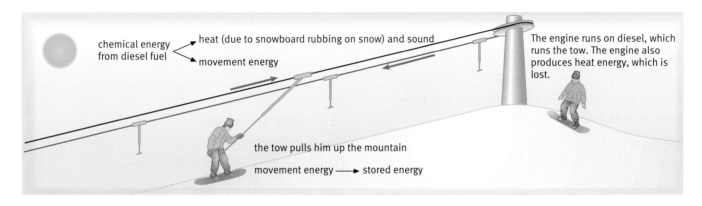

1 Copy and complete using words from the Language bank: All living things need _____ for every activity they do. _____ is the energy source for green plants. The major source of energy for animals is food. Energy is measured in _____ (symbol __). Different foods contain different amounts of energy. We can show how much energy food has by _____ it and using the heat to warm water.

2 Where do most of the Earth's energy resources come from?

3 If you were to carry out an investigation to find out which of two foods contained the most energy by burning them:
   a What would you keep the same?
   b What would you change?
   c Why would it be a good idea to repeat readings?
   d Are there any improvements you would make to the method of investigating energy in food shown above?

4 Burning fuels can harm the environment. Find out how this may happen and what we can do to reduce the harmful effects of fuels.

Language bank

burning
chemical energy
energy
energy transfer
joules (J)
kilojoule
movement energy
photosynthesis
respiration
stored energy
sunlight

Checkpoint

1 True or false?

Decide whether the following statements are true or false. Write down the true ones. Correct the false ones before you write them down.

a We burn fuels to release energy so we can make things happen.

b Food is not a type of fuel.

c We use lots of fuels to heat things, make things and move things.

d We make most of our electricity without burning fuels.

2 Renewable or not?

Sort the fuels below into two lists headed **renewable** and **non-renewable**. Use a different colour for each list. Try to think of some more fuels to add to your lists.

biomass
coal
fossil fuels
wood
gas
coke
petrol
kerosene

3 Energy transfers

Look at the energy transfers below. Choose the correct one for each device. Copy the energy transfers and draw a quick sketch of the device alongside each.

Energy transfers

chemical energy → heat energy + light energy + sound energy

chemical energy → movement energy + heat energy + sound energy

light energy → chemical energy

electrical energy → sound energy

Devices

pot plant   firework
personal stereo   car

4 Where our energy comes from

Match up the beginnings and endings to make complete sentences. Use a different colour to write each sentence.

Beginnings

Our main source of energy on Earth
Plants convert light energy to chemical energy
Animals get their energy
The energy in fuels

Endings

from eating plants (or other animals).
is the Sun.
came from the Sun.
when they make food by photosynthesis.

5 Choose the answer

Copy and complete this sentence, choosing the correct ending from the list below.

Renewable energy resources such as solar power, wind power, and hydroelectric power

are smelly and cause pollution.
can be used to generate electricity.
are using up our fossil fuels.
are useful fuels for cars.

6 Mind map

Draw a mind map using the following words. Add more words where you want.

Sun
fuels
energy
energy transfers*
renewable energy resources*
renewable fuels*
non-renewable
fossil fuels*
photosynthesis
plants
animals
*add examples of these

Electrical circuits

Before starting this unit, you should already be familiar with these ideas from earlier work.

○ Electrical devices and batteries can be connected in a circuit. What do we have to make sure of for the circuit to work?
○ We represent circuits with circuit diagrams.
○ We use symbols to show a battery, a bulb and a switch. Can you draw a circuit containing these things?

You will meet these key ideas as you work through this unit. Have a quick look now, and at the end of the unit read through them slowly.

○ An electrical circuit needs an energy source, such as a **cell** or **battery** to provide energy. This is connected to **components** such as a bulb or buzzer by wires, forming a complete circuit.
○ The cell converts chemical energy into electrical energy. This pushes **current** around the circuit. The current takes energy to the components.
○ The **voltage** is the amount of push in the circuit. A battery with a high voltage can push a bigger current around.
○ In the components, electrical energy is transferred. A bulb transfers electrical energy into light energy, along with some heat. A buzzer transfers electrical energy to sound energy, and a motor transfers electrical energy to movement energy.
○ In a **series circuit**, there is only one route for the current. The current is the same all the way around the circuit.
○ In a **parallel circuit**, there is more than one route for the current. There may be a different current in each loop if the components are different.

Circuit training

○ How do electrical circuits work?

We use electricity every day of our lives in things like phones, kettles, toasters, light bulbs, and computers. But electrical **equipment** or **devices** will only work if they are part of a **complete circuit**.

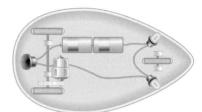

What is a complete circuit?

To make electrical things work, you need:

1 a **power supply**
   This could be a **cell** (battery), a lab pack, or a mains supply.

2 **wires** or **leads** to allow electrical charge to pass through
   These are always made of **conducting** material like copper.

3 an electrical **device**, like a bulb or a motor
   These **components** (parts) must be connected up to make a complete circuit. Electrical charge must be able to flow completely around the circuit, without any breaks or gaps in it. The flow of electric charge is known as **current**.

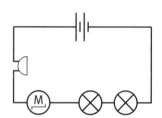

Symbols and circuits

We use an international shorthand system of **symbols** to represent the various part of an electric circuit. This is a lot easier than drawing every single battery or switch and ensures that everyone understands exactly what components are in the circuit.

A circuit diagram is a simplified sketch of the real circuit.

Component	Use	Circuit symbol
cell (battery)	provides energy to the circuit	
lead or wire	allows charge to travel through it	
bulb or filament lamp	converts electrical energy into heat and light energy	
resistor (fixed)	resists the flow of charge	
switch open	breaks the circuit and stops the electric current	
switch closed	turns circuit on	
power supply/lab pack	alternative to batteries	
ammeter	measures current	
motor	converts electrical energy into movement energy	
voltmeter	measures voltage	
buzzer	converts electrical energy into sound energy	

How to connect up a complete circuit

All batteries have a **positive** (+) end and a **negative** (−) end. These are called **poles** or **terminals**.

1 Attach a lead to the positive pole of the battery.
2 Connect the other end of this lead to a component. If the component has a + or − side, go into it through the + side and out through the − side.
3 Attach another lead, joining the component to the negative pole of the battery, or to another component.
4 Ensure that there is a continuous loop, including the components and battery.

What's wrong with my circuit?

Don't make these basic mistakes:

1 Circuit incomplete
Wires not connected to the battery or other device. This prevents the current flowing completely around the circuit.
Wire or lead is broken, or a connection is loose, so the current can't flow around the circuit.

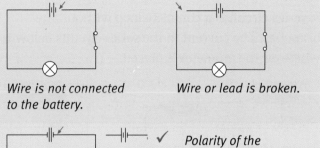

Wire is not connected to the battery.

Wire or lead is broken.

2 Polarity of the batteries incorrect
Arrange the poles of the batteries positive to negative (not positive to positive or negative to negative).

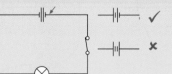

Polarity of the batteries is incorrect.

If a circuit isn't working here's how to check why:

1 Trace your finger round the circuit. If there are gaps, the circuit is incomplete.
2 Check that the battery polarity is correct.
3 Ask your teacher to check that the battery is OK and not dead.
4 Check that the bulb or one of the other components hasn't blown. You can usually see if the filament of a bulb has blown.

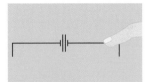
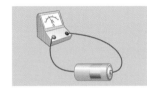

1 Copy and complete using words from the Language bank: A _____ is a material that allows electricity to pass through it. When the _____ is closed the circuit is complete; when it is open the circuit is broken and the flow of electric _____ stops. Circuits can be drawn using simple diagrams, using symbols to show the _____.

2 The front light of your bike does not work. Using your knowledge of circuits, describe what you would do to find the fault.

3 Why doesn't a bulb work when the filament inside it is broken?

4 Make a list of 10 different switches that you find at home.

Language bank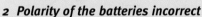

battery (cell)
bulb
circuit
components
conductor
current
filament
negative
polarity
positive
resistor
switch
symbol

O What happens in a circuit?

When a motor runs or a bulb shines we say that current is **flowing** in the circuit.

An ammeter.

Current is measured in **amps (A)**, which is short for **amperes**.

A **series circuit** is a complete loop without any branches. The current in the series circuits below is the same wherever the ammeter is placed.

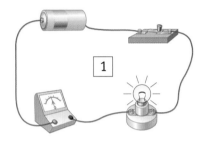

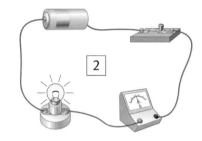

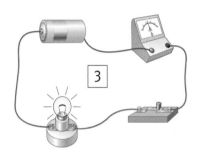

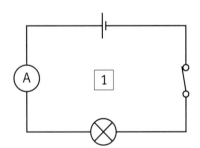

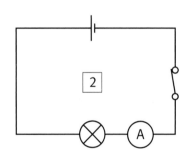

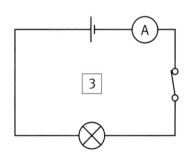

In circuits 1, 2 and 3, all ammeters give the same reading, so the current is not 'used up' by the components in the circuit.

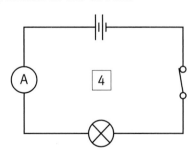

Circuit 4 has more batteries, which gives a bigger 'push' to the current. So the ammeter reading is higher and the bulb is brighter than in circuits 1, 2 and 3.

Too many batteries could blow the bulb – so watch out!

The current model

We sometimes use water flowing in pipes to picture what's happening in an electrical circuit. It's not a perfect **model**, but it helps to explain this bit:

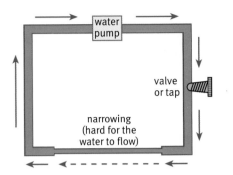
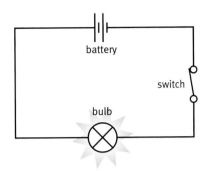

Water pipes can be used to explain how current moves round an electrical circuit.

In very narrow pipes, the water finds it hard to move because the pipe resists the flow of water. In electrical circuits, a **resistor** (or something that causes **resistance**), does a similar thing to the current.

In a filament bulb, the thin wires resist the current, become red or white hot and glow, giving out light.

Current flow depends on the components

The motor has a bigger resistance than the bulb, so the current is less in that circuit. The nature and number of components in a circuit will affect current flow and the ammeter reading will be different.

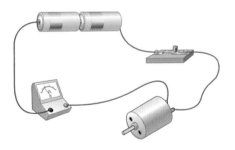
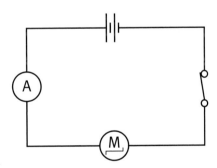

Change the component and you usually change the current flow.

So is there less current at the 'end' of the circuit?

No, it's the same. Current doesn't get used up like that.

1 Copy and complete using words from the Language bank: Current in a circuit is not used up by the components in it, but the _____ of components in a circuit affects current flow. Current is measured with an _____. Its units are _____ (__).

2 What is wrong with connecting the batteries as shown in the diagram opposite? Describe the correct way to connect them.

3 Why do you think that the motor has a bigger resistance than the bulb?

Language bank

ammeter
amps (A)
circuit
component
model
resistance
resistor
series

What happens in parallel circuits?

In **parallel circuits** the current has a 'choice' of routes it can take.

In the circuit diagram below, there is a total of 4 A of current. This 4 A divides up, so that 1 A of it goes on route 1 (through three bulbs) and the 3 A left goes on route 2 (through just one bulb).

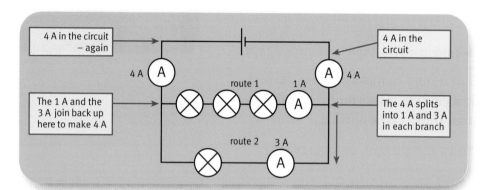

Series circuits are a bit like motor racing circuits and parallel circuits are a bit like normal roads with junctions.

As the current is not used up, the current 'joins up' again to produce the 4 A we started with.

The current in individual branches is different as this depends on what components are in the branch. The important thing to remember is that the current is not used up.

More about parallel circuits

Look at the parallel circuit below. If we turned on switches 1, 2 and 3 in turn and measured the current each time, we'd find that the current would go up.

The additional current would be used to light the additional bulb and all bulbs would have the same brightness.

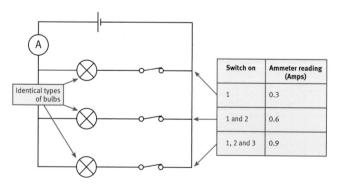

Switch on	Ammeter reading (Amps)
1	0.3
1 and 2	0.6
1, 2 and 3	0.9

With all switches closed, the sum of the current flowing in each branch (1, 2 and 3) is the same as that flowing in the main circuit.

In a series circuit the current is the same everywhere. If additional bulbs are added, there is more resistance so the current is reduced. This is why the bulbs get dimmer when more are added.

Series or parallel?

Series circuits are easy to understand. But if one component breaks or a connection is loose, the whole lot goes off, which is not very practical.

Christmas trees lights are sometimes series circuits – remove one bulb and they all go out.

Parallel circuits are a bit more complex. But the beauty of them is that you can turn one part of a parallel circuit on or off.

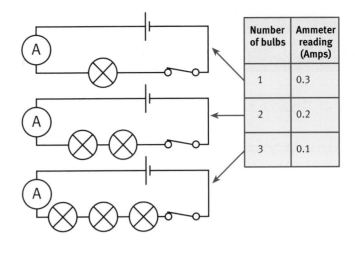

Number of bulbs	Ammeter reading (Amps)
1	0.3
2	0.2
3	0.1

Type of circuit	Series	Parallel
circuit	continuous	branched
current	same in all parts	different, depending on components (but add up current in branches and it will equal current in main circuit)
use	all on or off	parts can be on or off

A series circuit.

1 Copy and complete using words from the Language bank: Parallel circuits contain branches down which the _____ splits. The current in a branch depends on the electrical _____ in that part of the circuit, but the current in all the branches together is the same as the current in the main circuit.

2 Use your knowledge of parallel and series circuits to predict the reading on the ammeter X and Y and then R and S in the diagrams.

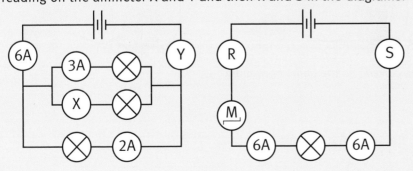

What do batteries do?

The battery converts the **chemical energy** stored inside it to **electrical energy**. The chemical energy comes from the materials that the battery is made from.

chemical energy in battery → electrical energy in circuit

Chemical reactions in the battery 'push' the current around a circuit. The amount of push is measured in **volts (V)**. Here are some batteries showing their voltage.

So the current isn't used up, but the battery's energy is!

That's exactly it.

Which of these gives the biggest 'push'?

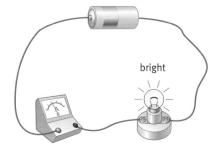

bright

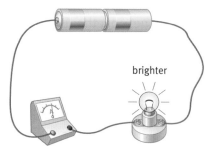

brighter

very bright

More batteries means a bigger push for the current, so the bulbs burn more brightly or the motor spins faster.

The larger the voltage of a battery (or the more batteries):
○ the larger the current in the circuit;
○ the brighter a bulb will burn, or the faster a motor will spin.

1.5 V dry cells.

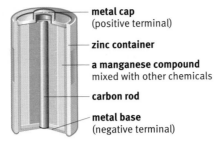
Inside one type of dry cell.

- metal cap (positive terminal)
- zinc container
- a manganese compound mixed with other chemicals
- carbon rod
- metal base (negative terminal)

A 12 V lead acid car battery.

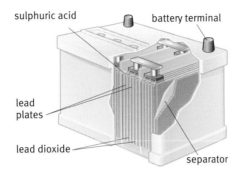
Inside a lead acid battery.

sulphuric acid
battery terminal
lead plates
lead dioxide
separator

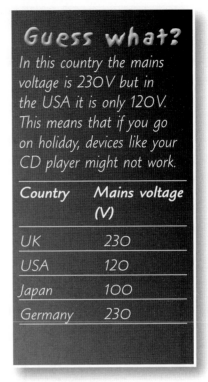

Guess what?

In this country the mains voltage is 230V but in the USA it is only 120V. This means that if you go on holiday, devices like your CD player might not work.

Country	Mains voltage (V)
UK	230
USA	120
Japan	100
Germany	230

A 12 volt car battery (lead acid) contains six 2 volt cells. These provide more 'push' than the 1.5 V dry cell battery you might use in a torch.

The batteries contain different chemicals and so provide a different voltage.

The components use up energy provided by the cells to provide us with heat, light, motion and sound. Eventually the cell's energy supply runs down.

A high current in amps (A) means a greater flow of electrical charge through the circuit. The current can be measured with an ammeter, which is placed in series in the circuit.

The more batteries in a circuit the higher the voltage. Voltmeters measure voltage (V) and are always placed in **parallel** around a component.

Electricity does not always come from batteries. If we plug something into a socket it uses **mains electricity**. This is brought to us along wires from power stations.

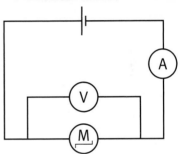
Ammeters are connected in series while voltmeters are connected in parallel.

1 Copy and complete using words from the Language bank: Electric _____ is the flow of charge in a circuit. Electricity may come from batteries. If we plug something into a wall socket we are using _____ _____.

2 What is the difference between voltage, volts and a voltmeter?

3 What is the difference between amps and an ammeter?

4 Where does the chemical energy found in a battery come from?

Language bank

- ammeter
- amps
- current
- mains electricity
- voltage
- voltmeter
- volts

O How can we explain what happens in electric circuits?

When you switch on a light, the 'electricity' in the wires is actually a flow of tiny particles around a circuit. These particles have a **negative charge**. We measure the amount of charge they carry in **coulombs (C)**.

We have already seen how the flow of current can be compared to the flow of water through pipes:

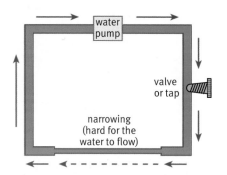

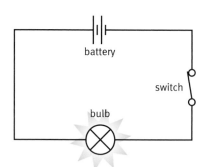

Electrical circuit	Water model
wires and leads	pipes
battery or cell	water pump
switch	valve or tap
electric charge	water
ammeter	flow meter
current	rate of flow
voltage	pressure difference
component that causes resistance like a bulb	narrowing

How the circuit compares to the water model.

A variable resistor like those found in dimmer switches can increase or decrease the **resistance** in the circuit. We can use the water model to explain how this works: the longer the narrowing of the water pipe, the lower the flow of water. In a circuit with a variable resistor, the higher the resistance, the lower the current – so the dimmer the bulb.

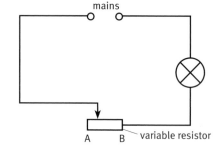

A dimmer switch dims the lights – just like a narrowing in a water pipe lowers the flow of water.

Parallel circuits

The water model can also help to explain what happens in parallel circuits. Each part of the pipe-work below has a similar component in the circuit.

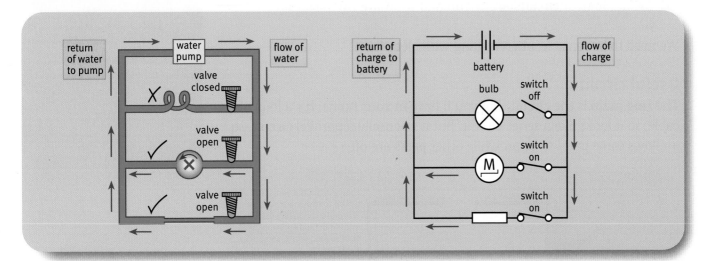

Models are not perfect

A model car is similar to a real car, but it has some obvious differences. So the model will not be perfect. Most scientific models are not perfect either, and also have their limitations.

We use models to:
o describe what we see happening in science;
o help us understand or imagine what's going on;
o help us predict what'll happen in the future.

The water flow model of electricity is good because it explains things like the fact that water flows back to the pump, like the current in a circuit.

But, the water model can't easily explain things like:
o how a loudspeaker works;
o how some sophisticated electronic circuits work;
o why electricity doesn't pour out when a circuit is broken – like water pipes would.

Hi-fi speakers contain parallel circuits.

1 Copy and complete using words from the Language bank: A _____ is something we use to help us understand scientific evidence. The _____ model is often used to help explain what goes on in circuits.

2 Which part of the water model acts like a switch in a circuit? List one similarity between these components, and one difference.

3 Why do you think the water model is used to explain circuits?

Language bank

coulomb (C)
dimmer switch
negative charge
variable resistor
water model

○ **What kinds of circuits are useful and what are the hazards?**

We need to be sensible when dealing with electricity.

Useful circuits

The **ring main** is the circuit that you'll have in your home. It's a loop of cable, so it looks like a series circuit. But it's actually a parallel circuit, so it allows some parts to be on while other parts are off.

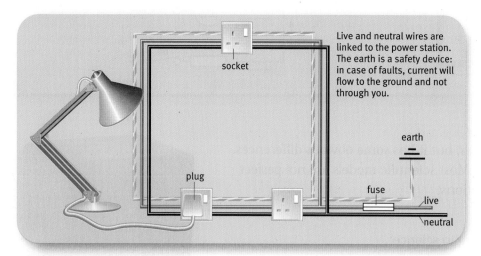

Live and neutral wires are linked to the power station. The earth is a safety device: in case of faults, current will flow to the ground and not through you.

A ring main circuit – how it works.

The two-way switch – doubly illuminating

A two-way switch lets you turn a light on at the bottom of the stairs and then turn it off when you get to the top. This might save you from falling down the stairs in the dark!

Fuses are safety devices

Sometimes a broken appliance takes more electricity than is safe, and could catch fire. To prevent this, plugs are fitted with **fuses**. A fuse is a thin piece of wire that melts when too much current flows through it. This breaks the circuit.

> **Guess what?**
> All the messages that your senses send to your brain go through nerves. The messages are really small electrical signals that tell your brain what's happening.

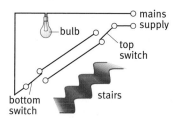

How a two-way switch works.

A three-pin plug. The fuse is coloured red.

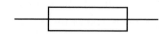

The symbol for a fuse.

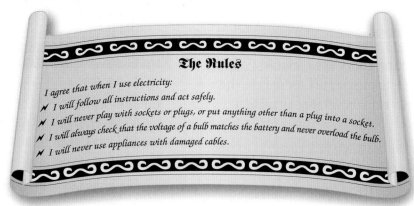

The Rules

I agree that when I use electricity:
- I will follow all instructions and act safely.
- I will never play with sockets or plugs, or put anything other than a plug into a socket.
- I will always check that the voltage of a bulb matches the battery and never overload the bulb.
- I will never use appliances with damaged cables.

Obey the rules or you could be sorry!

Hazards with electricity and mains

Mains electricity is quite safe if used properly. But it can be very dangerous if we're not careful. Can you spot the dangers in the picture below?

The short circuit

Electricity is lazy. It always takes the easiest route in a circuit. Unfortunately that might mean through you!

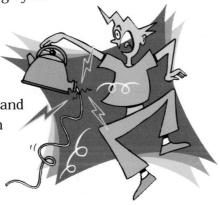

Sometimes a fault in an electric circuit allows the current to bypass part of a circuit. This may cause a large amount of current to flow, which can damage components and cause a fire. This is why plugs have an **earth** wire. The earth wire lets the current flow away into the ground, rather than through you.

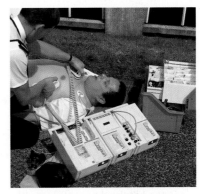

A defibrillator is a device that delivers a controlled electric shock to people who are having heart attacks. It helps to restore a natural heartbeat.

1 Copy and complete using words from the Language bank: The _____ _____ is a circuit found in the home. It's a ring of cables – one live, one _____ and one earth. Sockets are connected in _____ to this. When too much _____ flows through a circuit, the wire in the _____ will melt and break the circuit.

2 Find out the size of the correct fuse for the following. (Do not remove the casing of a plug without an adult present.)
   a an electric fan heater
   b a radio or CD player
   c a lamp

3 Why is it dangerous to use a hairdryer with wet hands?

4 Why is using mains electricity more dangerous than using batteries?

5 Find out what a pacemaker is used for and how it works.

6 Find out what electric fences are used for and how they work.

Language bank

current
earth wire
fuse
live wire
neutral wire
parallel
ring main
short circuit
two-way switch

Checkpoint

1 Connecting up

Copy and complete this sentence, choosing the correct ending from the list below.

To make an electrical component work, you need to connect it to

a battery, a lab pack and a switch.

a battery, conducting wires and a motor.

a power supply and conducting wires in a complete circuit.

a bulb and conducting wires in a complete circuit.

2 True or false?

Decide whether the following statements are true or false. Write down the true ones. Correct the false ones before you write them down.

a A cell converts chemical energy into heat energy.

b A cell pushes sultanas around the circuit.

c A current is a flow of electrical charges round the circuit.

d The wires used in a circuit must be good conductors of sound.

3 Bright lights

Here are some lists of components to make a series circuit. All the batteries and bulbs are the same. Sketch a circuit diagram for each, and say which circuit would give the brightest lights. What possible problem could happen with this circuit?

Components

a battery, a switch and one bulb

two batteries, a switch and one bulb

two batteries, a switch and two bulbs

three batteries, a switch and one bulb

4 Series and parallel circuits

Here is a list of sentences. You are going to make two lists, series (red) and parallel (green). Write each sentence below in the correct list. Draw a circuit diagram showing an example of each type of circuit.

There is only one route for the current.

There is a choice of routes for the current.

The current may vary through components in different branches.

The current is the same through all the components.

The sum of the current in each branch is the same as the current in the main circuit.

Christmas tree lights all go off when one bulb blows.

Christmas tree lights don't all go off when one bulb blows.

Components can be switched off separately.

Components cannot be switched off separately.

5 Energy transfers

Match up the energy transfers with the components. Use a different colour to write each component name, or draw its circuit symbol, along with its energy transfer.

Energy transfers

chemical energy → electrical energy

electrical energy → light energy

electrical energy → movement energy

electrical energy → sound energy

Components

motor

buzzer

bulb

cell

Forces and their effects

Before starting this unit, you should already be familiar with these ideas from earlier work.

○ A force may be big or small. A force may be a push or a pull. How would you place two magnets so that they pull on each other?

○ A force is measured using a forcemeter. Can you remember the units we use to measure forces?

○ If you drop a cup, it always falls downwards, not upwards or sideways. What is the name of the force that makes this happen?

○ There are two forces acting on a parachutist's body. Weight acts downwards. What force acts upwards?

You will meet these key ideas as you work through this unit. Have a quick look now, and at the end of the unit read through them slowly.

○ A **force** changes the shape, direction or speed of something. A force has **magnitude** (size) and direction.

○ If the forces on a stationary object are **balanced**, the object does not move. If you push your hands on both sides of a book with equal force, it will not move.

○ The forces on an object may change its shape. If you push down on a soft ball, it will get flatter.

○ If the forces on a stationary object are unbalanced, it will start to move. If you hit a snooker ball, it will start to move.

○ Unbalanced forces also affect a moving object. It could go faster, slow down, or change direction.

○ If an object is moving at a constant speed, the forces on it are balanced.

○ **Mass** is the amount of matter in an object, measured in kilograms. **Weight** is a force, which is caused by gravity acting on the object, and is measured in **newtons** (N).

○ **Friction** is a force that acts when surfaces move over each other. Air resistance is a kind of friction. Car brakes use friction to stop the car, and you can walk without slipping over all the time because of friction between your feet and the ground.

○ We can reduce friction between moving parts by **lubricating** them with oil or grease.

○ Where do we come across forces?

A force is a push or a pull. Forces can't be seen, but you can see what they do. For example:

a Forces can change the **shape** of things:

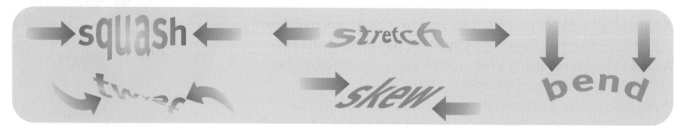

b Forces can change the **speed** of things:

c Forces can change the **direction** of things:

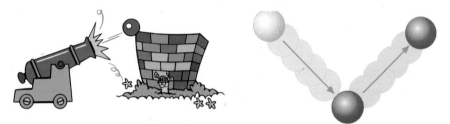

Types of force

Some forces act when things touch. These are called contact forces. Other forces act from a distance.

Forces act in one direction

Forces have a certain **size** and act in one **direction**. We use an **arrow** to show what direction a force is acting in. A **big** arrow means a **large** force.

If an object isn't moving then the forces on it are **balanced**. **Unbalanced** forces can change an object's speed or direction of motion.

No movement – equal (balanced) forces.

Unequal (unbalanced) forces – object moves to the left.

Unequal (unbalanced) forces – object moves to the right.

Forces add together (act like one bigger force) – object moves to the right.

How to measure forces

We use a **forcemeter** (newtonmeter) to measure the size of a force. The larger the force, the higher the reading on the forcemeter will be. Force is measured in **newtons** (N).

Some forcemeters look like bathroom scales and some look like fancy springs.

A forcemeter measures force in newtons.

1 Copy and complete using words from the Language bank: Most _____ are simply pushes or pulls, exerted by one thing on another. Forces have size and direction and can be shown by an arrow. Force is measured in _____ (__).

2 Name four different forces.

3 How could you measure the downward force an apple exerts?

Language bank

air resistance
forces
forcemeter
friction
gravity
magnetic force
newton (N)
newtonmeter

○ What does friction do?

Friction is a force that tries to stop two surfaces from moving over each other. Friction can be useful or it can be a nuisance.

Life without friction – unstoppable!

Cars would skid.

Knots would untie.

You would slip over!

Without friction
○ Car tyres would not be able to grip the road and their brakes wouldn't work.
○ Your shoes couldn't grip the floor and you'd be slipping all the time.
○ No knots would stay tied.
○ Riding a bike would be impossible – like riding on ice.

But friction can also be a nuisance, because:
○ It can heat things up which can damage machines.
○ It slows moving things down.

Reducing friction

Even the smoothest polished surfaces will have tiny bumps that act like microscopic bits of sandpaper. It's these bumps that cause friction between surfaces as they rub together.

The friction between two surfaces can be reduced using a **lubricant** like oil or grease. Putting a lubricant like oil on the surfaces moves them apart so they move over one another much more easily and don't wear away so quickly.

Air resistance

Air resistance (drag) is a kind of friction that drags against something moving through air – like you on your bicycle, or a car on the road. The more **streamlined** a vehicle is, the lower the drag, so the easier it can move through the air and the faster it can go.

The rally car's disc brakes glow red hot as a result of friction.

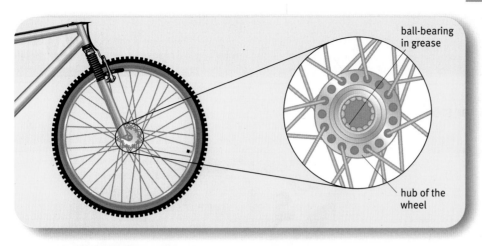

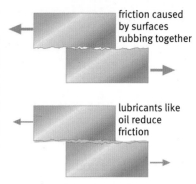

friction caused by surfaces rubbing together

lubricants like oil reduce friction

ball-bearing in grease

hub of the wheel

The inside of a mountain bike wheel hub. The wheel is mounted on small ball bearings which are packed with grease to help the wheel turn with as little friction as possible.

Even surfaces that seem smooth, like copper, have roughness, which causes friction. Oil helps to reduce friction.

As a car speeds up, the drag increases. Eventually the drag matches the thrust and the car can go no faster. It is at top speed.

With better streamlining the car can go even faster because more speed is needed to produce the same amount of drag.

Guess what?

Graphite, which is found in pencils, is a solid lubricant that stops surfaces from rubbing together. Try running a pencil down the hinge of a squeaky door – bingo, it stops squeaking.

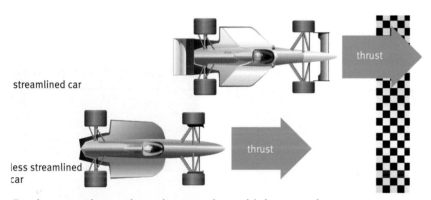

streamlined car

thrust

less streamlined car

thrust

For the same thrust, the red car reaches a higher speed.

TOP BRICKS
Dragstar

Dart- or wedge-shaped vehicles are streamlined; brick-shaped vehicles are not.

1 Copy and complete using words from the Language bank: _____ is a force that tries to stop movement. Friction acts between two surfaces and can be reduced using a _____. Air _____ or drag is a frictional force that acts against moving objects like cars. The more _____ an object, the lower its air resistance.

2 Why is a wet road more dangerous than a dry road for car drivers?

3 For some parts of a bicycle, friction is very important but for others it's a nuisance. List parts of a bicycle where:
   a friction is essential
   b friction must be reduced.

4 Fish are well adapted to reduce the resistance between their bodies and the water they swim in. Describe two adaptations.

Language bank

air resistance
drag
friction
lubricant
streamlined
thrust

○ What affects how quickly a car stops?

How quickly a car stops depends on:
- ○ the speed it's going;
- ○ the efficiency of its brakes;
- ○ what the road surface is like;
- ○ the air resistance slowing it down;
- ○ how long it takes the driver to apply the brakes.

Speed
Speed tells us how far you've gone and how long it took you.

speed = distance moved ÷ time taken

The unit we use to measure speed depends on what units of distance and time are used. Usually in science, distance is measured in **metres** and time in **seconds**:

speed = metres per second = metres/seconds = m/s

Maclaren F1 – the fastest production car.

Comparing speeds

Competitor	Speed (m/s)	Time to travel 100 m (sec)
snail	0.00006	still counting...
100 m world record holder	0.98	9.8 sec
Tour de France cyclist	14	7.1
fastest production car	102	0.98
jet fighter	943	0.11

Distance/time graphs
Distance/time graphs show a summary of a journey. The three graphs below show three possible patterns. In each case the slope is the speed.

Other units of speed: miles per hour (mph) kilometres per hour (km/h).

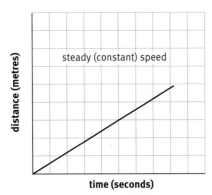

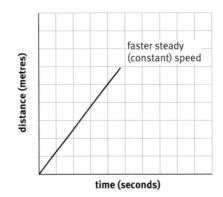

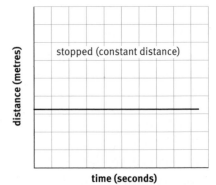

Graph A *The distance covered every single second is the same.*

Graph B *The distance covered every single second is the same, but greater than in Graph A.*

Graph C *The distance covered does not change as time goes on, so the object is not moving.*

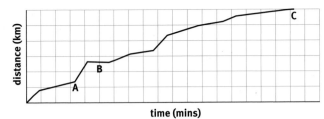

Distance/time graph for a journey home. What do you think is happening at points A, B, and C?

Frictional forces

To stop a car you apply the brakes. How quickly you stop depends on how much **frictional force** you can put on the brakes of the car, and how well the tyres grip the road. Most modern cars help the driver to amplify the force (make the force bigger) and some have anti-lock brakes.

If a vehicle is not streamlined the natural air resistance will slow it down but not quickly enough to stop in an emergency.

Thinking about stopping

The driver of a car must react to the situation on the road and think about what to do. This adds to the total time (and distance) it takes to stop. It is called **reaction time**.

mph	m/s	Thinking distance (metres)	Stopping distance (metres)	Total distance (metres)
30	13	9	14	23
40	18	12	24	36
50	22	15	38	53
60	27	18	55	73 (or 18 car lengths)

The driver applies a force to the brake pedal or lever, and a force is applied to the brake discs.

1 Copy and complete using words from the Language bank: _____ is a force that helps us move but also slows us down. _____ distances of vehicles are related to frictional forces and _____ time. _____ is how far you have travelled in a certain time. Its units are usually metres per _____ (in science lessons).

2 When braking, the thinking distance increases with speed. Explain why it's not the same for different speeds.

3 A reckless dog rollerblades down a street 50 m long in 5 seconds. Calculate its speed.

Language bank

distance
distance time graph
friction
kilometres per hour
metres per second
miles per hour
reaction time
speed
stopping distances
time

O Why do things float?

Things float because of **upthrust**. Have you ever tried to push a balloon or ball down into water? Upthrust is the upward force that acts on things in a liquid.

Upthrust keeps things afloat.

Gravity pulls all objects down towards the centre of the Earth (this pull is the **weight** of the object). Upthrust pushes upwards against the weight.

When the two forces are equal and balanced the object is stationary and floats.

An object floats in water, as the water provides upthrust.

If something is floating freely then the weight of water it **displaces** (pushes out of its way) is equal to its own weight.

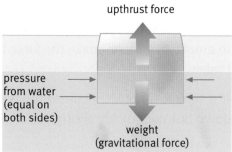

upthrust force

pressure
from water
(equal on
both sides)

weight
(gravitational force)

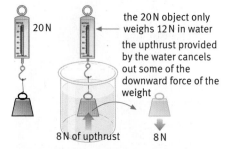

the 20 N object only
weighs 12 N in water

the upthrust provided
by the water cancels
out some of the
downward force of the
weight

8 N of upthrust   8 N

The upthrust provided by the water cancels out some of the downward force of the weight, so the object seems to weigh less in water.

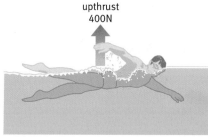

upthrust
400N

weight of water displaced = 400N

The weight of the water displaced is the weight of the swimmer.

Density

Density is all about how **heavy** something is for its **size**. You work it out like this:

density = mass ÷ volume

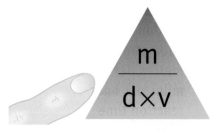

$$\frac{m}{d \times v}$$

Put your finger over d to find the formula.

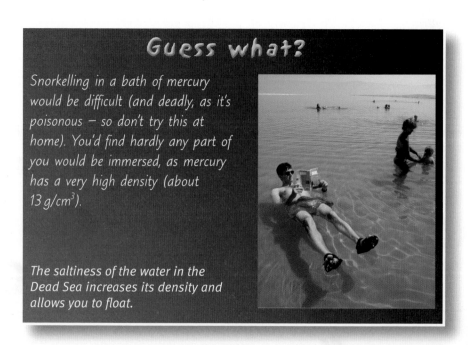

Guess what?

Snorkelling in a bath of mercury would be difficult (and deadly, as it's poisonous – so don't try this at home). You'd find hardly any part of you would be immersed, as mercury has a very high density (about 13 g/cm^3).

The saltiness of the water in the Dead Sea increases its density and allows you to float.

Find the density of gold

1 Write out the formula:

density = mass ÷ volume

$d = m \div v$

mass = 19.3g

balance

2 Find out the mass and volume:

Use a mass balance to find the mass. Measure the volume of a solid by putting it into an Archimedes can. The volume of water that pours out is the volume of the block.

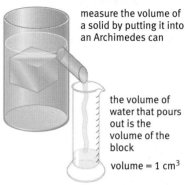

measure the volume of a solid by putting it into an Archimedes can

the volume of water that pours out is the volume of the block

volume = 1 cm³

3 Work out the density:

Put the numbers from the diagram in the equation:

$d = ?$ unknown (that's what we're working out)

$m = 19.3$ g (from the balance)

$v = 1$ cm³ (measure with a ruler or work out using Archimedes' can)

$d = m \div v$

$d = 19.3$ g $\div$ 1 cm³

$d = 19.3$ g/cm³

More densities

Things float in water only if their density is lower than (or equal to) that of water.

Substance	Density (g/cm³)	Will it float in water?
gold	19.3	✗
aluminium	2.7	✗
wood	0.75	✓
oil	0.8	✓
steel	8.0	✗
air	0.0013	✓
silver	10.5	✗

Density of water = 1 g/cm³ so 1 cm³ has a mass of 1 g

The hot air is less dense than the cold air so the balloons rise.

1 Copy and complete using words from the Language bank: When objects are immersed in water an _____ (upward force) acts on them. The upthrust is equal to the _____ of the object. Upthrust is different in different liquids. When an object is stationary the forces on it are _____. _____ is mass divided by volume.

2 Steel doesn't float in water, so how come steel ships float?

3 Using your knowledge of density, how could you tell if a king's crown was pure gold and not a cheaper metal?

Language bank

balanced forces
density
displace
float
g/cm³
gravity
mass
upthrust
volume
weight

Weight in science

O What is weight?

In the list below the word **weight** is confused with the word **mass**.

> **Lose pounds at Weight Watchers!**
> **Do you want to weigh 50 kg?**

> Mass is the amount of matter in an object and is measured in kilograms.
>
> Weight is a force and is measured in newtons.

> 1 kilogram = 1 kg
>
> 1 kg is equivalent to 10 N
>
> where N = newton

The mass of the ski diver is pulled to the Earth by the force of gravity. His mass does not change wherever he is, but his weight does.

The **force of gravity** pulls downwards on the mass of the 1 kg ball with a gravitational force of 10 N, towards the centre of the Earth.

The 2 kg ball has more matter in it, so the matter is pulled down to the Earth's centre with a larger force – 20 N.

There's a link between mass and weight but they are different. But you must admit, 'weighing' something sounds so much better than 'massing' something...?

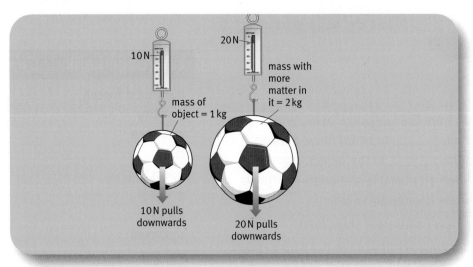

20 N

10 N

mass with more matter in it = 2 kg

mass of object = 1 kg

10 N pulls downwards

20 N pulls downwards

Gravity

Gravity is the **force of attraction** between objects that have mass. The bigger the object, the larger the gravitational force of attraction.

Even small masses will attract each other – just not very much.

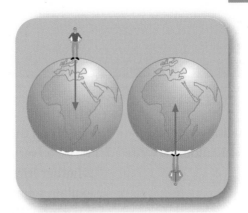

The mass of an object on Earth is attracted to the centre of the Earth by gravity. The force arrow points towards its centre – wherever you are.

Weight can change

Weight is caused by gravity acting on a mass. Since gravity can change, so can weight. Gravity and therefore weight depend on where you are in the Universe.

Where	In Space	Sea of Tranquility (Moon)	Ramsbottom (Earth)	near Jupiter
Mass	35 kg	35 kg	35 kg	35 kg
Weight	0 N	59 N	350 N	800 N

1 Copy and complete using words from the Language bank: Mass is the amount of _____ in an object and is measured in _____. Weight is a force and is measured in _____. Weight is caused by _____ acting on a mass. Since gravity can change, weight can also change.

2 Why did astronauts who walked on the Moon wear heavy boots? (Clue: it wasn't a fashion statement...)

3 Imagine that gravity on the Earth was similar to that on the Moon. Describe your journey to school.

Language bank

force of attraction
gravity
kilograms
mass
matter
newtons
weight

Checkpoint

1 What is a force?
Match up the beginnings and endings to make complete sentences. Use a different colour to write each sentence.

Beginnings
A force changes
A force has magnitude
A force is drawn
A force is measured

Endings
the shape, speed or direction of something.
as a force arrow.
in newtons.
and direction.

2 True or false?
Decide whether the following statements are true or false. Write down the true ones. Correct the false ones before you write them down.
a If a toy truck is not moving, the forces on it are balanced.
b If an unbalanced force acts on the toy truck, it will start to complain.
c If the toy truck is already moving and a force acts on it, its colour will change.
d If the toy truck is moving at a steady speed, friction equals the pushing force.

3 Mass and weight
Copy and complete these sentences, unscrambling the words.

Mass is the amount of **tartem** in an object, measured in **olmargski**.
Weight is a **refoc**, measured in **wennsot**.
Weight is caused by the force of **trygiva** acting on the mass.
Gravity is smaller on the Moon, so your **thegwi** on the Moon would be less than on Earth.

4 Friction
Match up the types of friction and the examples. Write a (very) short story for each one saying whether friction is useful or not. If it is useful, explain what would happen without it, or draw a cartoon. If it is not useful, say how we can reduce it.

Friction forces
o air resistance of a parachute through air
o air resistance of a car
o friction between the soles of your trainers and the road
o friction between bicycle brakes and wheels
o friction between moving parts of machinery

Examples
o you complete the London Marathon in under four hours
o pistons and cylinders inside a car engine
o a skydiver falls to Earth safely
o you speed down the hill and meet a tractor blocking the road
o the top speed of a Boxtop 1.2 is lower than that of a Flowline 1.2 although they have the same engine

6 Mind map
Draw a mind map using the following words. Add more words where you want.

forces
balanced
unbalanced
weight
gravity
magnetic
friction
air resistance
newtons

The Solar System and beyond

Before starting this unit, you should already be familiar with these ideas from earlier work.

- The Earth, Moon and Sun are roughly spherical. The Earth goes round the Sun, and the Moon goes round the Earth. About how long does it take for the Moon to orbit the Earth once?
- The position of the Sun in the sky changes through the day. Where do we see it in the morning, and in the evening?
- The Earth spins on its axis. Which way does our part of the Earth face when it is daylight?
- The Earth takes a year to orbit the Sun once. Write down two things that we notice changing in the UK during this cycle.

You will meet these key ideas as you work through this unit. Have a quick look now, and at the end of the unit read through them slowly.

- The Earth spins on its axis. One full turn takes a **day**.
- The Earth orbits the Sun. Each orbit takes **one year**.
- The Earth's axis is tilted. This means we notice **seasonal changes** during the year, as the Earth orbits the Sun.
- When the northern hemisphere is tilted towards the Sun, we have **summer**. When the northern hemisphere is tilted away from the Sun, we have **winter**.
- The Sun is a **star**. It gives out light. The Earth and other planets, along with the Moon, do not give out their own light. We can see them because they reflect the light from the Sun.
- An **eclipse** happens when a shadow hides our view of something.
- In our **Solar System**, there are nine planets orbiting the Sun: Mercury, Venus, Earth, Mars, Jupiter, Saturn, Uranus, Neptune, and Pluto.

○ **What is the cause of a year, a month, a day?**
○ **What causes the seasons on Earth?**

The Sun seems to move across the sky throughout the day. The reason for this is that the Earth is actually spinning round (**rotating**) on its **axis**.

Dawn to dusk.

Day and night

The Earth spins through one complete rotation in 24 hours. Day is when the part of the Earth you're on faces the Sun, and night is when the part of the Earth you're on faces away from the Sun.

The rotation of the Earth also makes the stars appear to move across the sky.

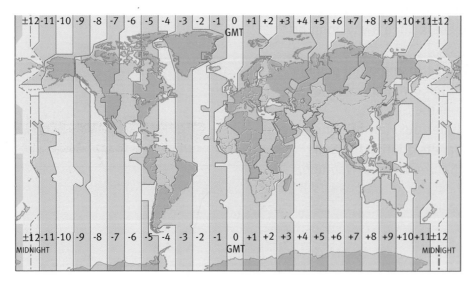

Orbits

As well as rotating on its axis, the Earth moves round the Sun. Its path is called an **orbit**. It takes a year (about 365 days) for one orbit to be completed. In a similar way, the Moon orbits the Earth. Other things in space, like planets and satellites, also move in orbits.

Guess what?

The Sun is not solid and the middle spins faster than the poles. This might be hard to picture, but the Sun's equator rotates completely in 25 Earth days, whereas the poles take 27 days. Imagine if this happened on Earth!

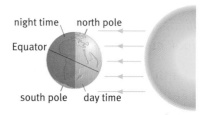

Earth rotates anticlockwise

The world is divided into 24 time zones. The time in each zone differs from the zone on either side by one hour. When you travel west you put your watch back an hour for every time zone you cross. When you travel east you add an hour for each zone.

A month

It takes about 28 days for the Moon to orbit the Earth. The same side of the Moon always faces the Earth. We never see the other side, or dark side, of the Moon.

We all know that a calendar month is 30 or 31 days, except in February, which has 28 or 29 days. A lunar or Moon month is always 28 days long (27 days, 7 hours and 2.8 seconds to be exact).

Seasons

The Earth's axis is tilted at an angle. The way the Earth is tilted as it orbits the Sun determines how much sunlight different places get. When the northern hemisphere is tilted towards the Sun, more of the northern hemisphere is in sunlight than in darkness. In Britain and other parts of the northern hemisphere days are long and nights are short – we have **summer**.

When the northern hemisphere is tilted away from the Sun, less of the northern hemisphere is in Sunlight than darkness, so days are short and nights are long – we have **winter**.

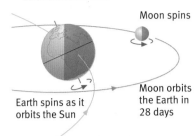

Earth orbits the Sun

Moon spins

Earth spins as it orbits the Sun

Moon orbits the Earth in 28 days

The Moon takes a month to orbit the Earth.

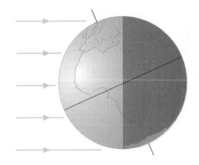

Summer in the northern hemisphere.

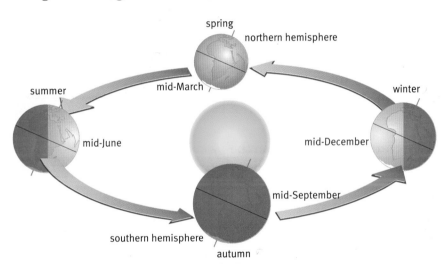

The four seasons.

1. Copy and complete using words from the Language bank: It takes 365 days for the Earth to _____ the Sun. During _____ the Earth tilts towards the Sun, and during _____ the Earth tilts away from the Sun.

2. Explain how day and night occur.

3. In the summer in Finland, it never becomes properly dark at night. But in winter, they have periods of very short days and some places are in darkness 24 hours a day. Using diagrams, explain why nights are long in Finland in the winter.

4. Describe what happens to the Moon during a month.

Language bank

axis
day
equator
lunar
model
night
northern hemisphere
orbit
season
summer
time zone
winter

139

How do we see the Sun and the Moon?

Twinkle, twinkle

The famous nursery rhyme gives us a clue as to what's up there in the night sky.

If you're unsure if a **celestial body** is a **planet** or a **star**, just see if it **twinkles** or not. Stars **emit** (give off) light and appear to twinkle. Planets **reflect** light from the Sun. They rarely twinkle.

> *Twinkle twinkle little star*
> *How I wonder what you are.*
> *Up above the sky so bright...*

A **luminous** object gives out light. It's what we call a **light source**. Non-luminous objects can reflect light, but are not light sources.

The Sun is a light source

The Sun is a star and therefore a source of light. The Moon and Earth are not. They are only seen by the light that they reflect (reflected light).

We see the Moon because the light rays emitted by the Sun travel in straight lines through space and bounce off the Moon.

Luminous objects.

Phases of the Moon

The Moon is known as a **natural satellite** because it moves around the Earth. Our view of it changes daily, as it moves. The sequence is the same each month. We call this pattern the **phases of the Moon**.

Non-luminous objects.

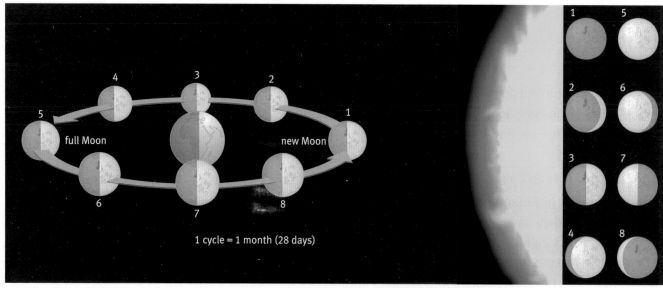

full Moon   new Moon

1 cycle = 1 month (28 days)

The phases of the Moon viewed from Earth. Would you see phases of the Earth from the Moon?

Eclipses

Eclipse of the Moon

When the Earth passes between the Sun and the Moon, a shadow covers the Moon. This is a **lunar eclipse**.

Eclipse of the Sun

When the Moon passes between the Earth and the Sun, sunlight is blocked off, casting a shadow on the Earth.

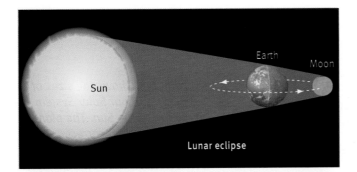

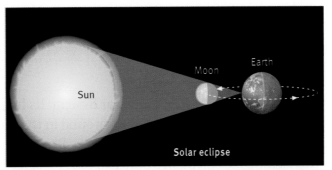

The start of a lunar eclipse.

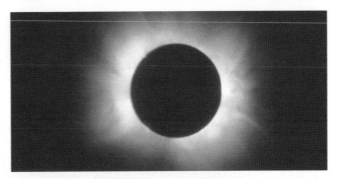

A solar eclipse. Solar eclipses should be viewed through special filters designed to protect your eyes. Never look directly at the Sun, even very quickly – it could blind you.

Using evidence about eclipses

Eclipses confirm a number of facts, such as:

1 The Moon orbits around the Earth.
2 The Earth orbits around the Sun.
3 Light from the Sun travels in straight lines.
4 The Moon is smaller than the Sun.
5 The Moon is closer to the Earth than the Sun.

---

1 Copy and complete using words from the Language bank: Objects are either _____ (they give out light) or non-luminous (they only reflect light). The _____ is a light source, but the Moon and Earth are only seen by reflected light. The view of the Moon from the Earth changes in a regular pattern, which is known as the _____ of the Moon.

2 Describe how an eclipse of the Sun occurs.

3 Describe how an eclipse of the Moon occurs.

4 Why is a new Moon difficult to see?

5 How does a solar eclipse show that light travels in straight lines?

6 Imagine you were watching the solar eclipse of summer 1999. Write a short report describing what it was like.

Language bank

emit
light source
luminous
lunar eclipse
Moon
non-luminous
phases
reflect
solar eclipse
Sun

Where we live

O What does the Solar System consists of?

The solar system consists of a collection of **planets**, **moons**, **asteroids**, and a **star**, which we call the **Sun**.

Our local neighbourhood

The Sun is at the centre of our Solar System. Its huge mass attracts the planets and the big rocks that float around in the asteroid belt. They are held by the Sun's strong gravity in **orbits**. Planets' orbits are nearly circular, and most asteroids have **elliptical** (oval) orbits.

This diagram shows the sizes of the planets in our Solar System compared to the Sun. The planets are shown in their correct order from the Sun, but the distances between them are not to scale.

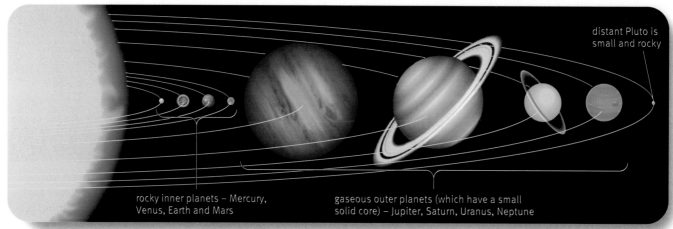

distant Pluto is small and rocky

rocky inner planets – Mercury, Venus, Earth and Mars

gaseous outer planets (which have a small solid core) – Jupiter, Saturn, Uranus, Neptune

Mercury

Venus

Earth

Mars

Jupiter

Saturn

Uranus

Neptune

Pluto

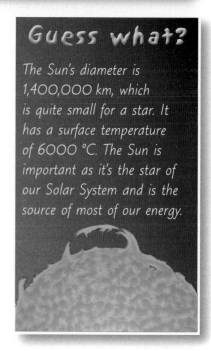

Guess what?

The Sun's diameter is 1,400,000 km, which is quite small for a star. It has a surface temperature of 6000 °C. The Sun is important as it's the star of our Solar System and is the source of most of our energy.

The nine planets in our Solar System – not to scale. Look at the Solar System picture for the sizes.

By making observations with telescopes scientists have been able to tell us about the other planets. Conditions are very different from those on Earth. One very important condition is **temperature**. The **distance** of a planet from the Sun and the nature of the planet's **atmosphere** have an important effect on the planet's temperature.

The atmosphere and surface temperature of most of the other planets are too harsh (too hot or too cold) for human life. The force of **gravity** is also different on other planets. On larger planets like Jupiter, for example, the force of gravity is larger, so you'd feel heavier. To cap it all – on Pluto, you'd have a birthday only once every 248 years!

Planet	Diameter (compared to Earth)	Average distance from Sun (million km)	Mass (compared to Earth)	Time to go around the Sun (Earth days or years)	Average temperature (°C)	Atmosphere – main gases	No. of moons
Mercury	0.4	58	0.05	88 days	350	no atmosphere	0
Venus	0.9	108	0.8	228 days	480	carbon dioxide & sulphuric acid	0
Earth	1	150	1	365 days	20	nitrogen/oxygen	1
Mars	0.5	228	0.1	687 days	−23	carbon dioxide	2
Jupiter	11	778	318	12 years	−150	hydrogen, helium, ammonia, methane	39
Saturn	9.4	1430	95	29 years	−190	hydrogen & helium	31
Uranus	4.0	2870	15	84 years	−210	hydrogen, helium, ammonia, methane	23
Neptune	3.8	4500	17	165 years	−220	hydrogen, helium, methane	8
Pluto	0.2	5900	0.003	248 years	−240	nitrogen/ice & rock surface	1

1 Copy and complete using words from the Language bank: Our _____ System includes the Sun, its nine _____, the asteroids and the natural _____ of the planets. Planets orbit the Sun just like the _____ orbits the Sun.

2 List the nine planets and asteroid belt in order from the Sun and make up a sentence or rhyme (mnemonic) to help you remember the correct order, e.g. **M**y **V**ery **E**ager **M**onkey....

3 Why is the Earth attracted to the Sun?

4 What is the difference between a moon and the Moon?

5 What is the link between the distance a planet is from the Sun and the length of its year. (Tip: The larger the distance...)

Language bank

asteroid	orbit
atmosphere	planets
Earth	Pluto
galaxy	satellites
Jupiter	Saturn
Mars	Solar System
Mercury	Uranus
Moon	Venus
Neptune	

○ What is beyond the Solar System?

The **Universe** is made up of millions of **galaxies**. Our galaxy is called the **Milky Way** and is made up of millions of stars, one of which we call the Sun. Around the Sun orbit the nine planets, asteroids, and the many comets that make up our Solar System.

asteroid

Moon

planet

Sun (a star)

Solar System

galaxy   Universe

Halley's Comet, last seen in 1986, is due to reappear in 2061.

Most asteroids orbit the Sun in the asteroid belt between Jupiter and Mars.

A roving vehicle exploring the planet Mars.

The central region of the Milky Way, the galaxy that is home to our Solar System.

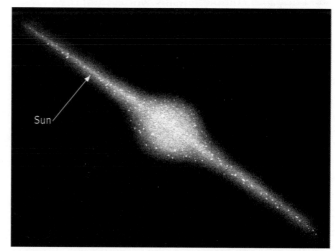

Sun

A diagram showing a side-on view of the Milky Way. The position of the Sun is indicated by the arrow.

Light travels at 300 million metres per second. A **light year** is the distance that light travels in one year.

Beyond the Solar System

The stars we see at night are mainly those near to us in the Milky Way. But other stars are spread throughout the universe. Most of them almost certainly have their own cluster of planets and form their own solar systems, which make up millions of galaxies.

The Milky Way is a **spiral galaxy** like the one below. Our galaxy is about 900,000 light years wide.

As the Earth rotates the stars seem to move across the sky.

The nearest galaxy to us is Andromeda, 2 million light years away. When we look at the stars in Andromeda we are looking back in time, as the light has taken 2 million years to reach us.

No one is quite sure how big the Universe is, but it's so big you can't imagine how big it is and research suggests it's getting bigger, like an inflating balloon.

This photograph of a group of galaxies was taken by the Hubble Space Telescope.

A spiral galaxy. The central region contains mostly older stars; in the outer region are younger, blue stars.

1 Copy and complete using words from the Language bank: Studying the planets and stars has helped us to build up a picture of our _____ System and our galaxy, which is called the _____ _____. The _____ is made up of millions of galaxies.

2 Put the following in order of size from smallest to largest: Moon, Solar System, planet, galaxy, asteroid, Universe, Sun

3 At present the Earth is the only planet within our Solar System that is known to support life. Using the information in the table on page 143, explain why you think this is.

Language bank

- galaxy
- light year
- Milky Way
- Solar System
- stars
- telescope
- Universe

145

- What does the Solar System consist of?
- What is beyond the Solar System?

Astronomers and **astrophysicists** study the Solar System and the Universe and construct **models** that attempt to explain what they find. This is **astronomy**.

To find out more about the Solar System, **probes** are sent into space to visit other planets. Scientists also analyse the invisible light or **radiation** that is found in space. This gives us information about the conditions on planets, like how hot they are, and details about their chemical composition.

The Hubble telescope has helped astronomers see galaxies and star clusters in more detail than ever before.

William and Caroline Herschel – the astronomers and the telescope

'I have looked further into space than any human being did before me.'

William Herschel (1738–1822) and his sister Caroline (1750–1848) were originally from Germany but spent much of their lives living in Bath, in England. William was a professional musician, but began making his own telescopes as his interest in astronomy grew. He discovered the planet Uranus in

William Herschel – a top astronomer of his time. His sister Caroline also made an important contribution to astronomy.

1781. His work on the nature of nebulae (enormous clouds of stars like our own galaxy) and the structure of the Universe made him the first man to give a reasonably correct picture of the shape of our star-system which he called the Galaxy.

Caroline was his devoted assistant and herself discovered eight comets and published many important findings.

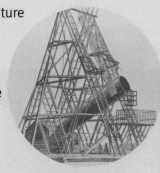

The telescope built by William Herschel in 1787–1789. The tube of the telescope was 12 metres long.

The William Herschel Telescope on La Palma in the Canary Islands is named after the great astronomer

What mysteries does the Universe hold?

Every planet in our Solar System, with the exception of Pluto, has been closely observed by a spacecraft.

For example, *Voyager 2* passed close to Jupiter in 1979 and is now on its way to the edge of our Solar System.

In 2004 the *Cassini* spacecraft will release a probe that will land on Titan, Saturn's largest moon. It will then beam back pictures and data about Titan and Saturn itself.

A photo taken from the Hubble telescope.

A computer artwork of the Cassini spacecraft, which was launched in 1997 and is expected to reach Saturn in 2004.

1 Copy and complete using words from the Language bank: _____ is the study of planets, stars and other solar systems and galaxies. William Herschel was a famous _____ who discovered the planet _____.

2 What is the difference between an astronaut, an astronomer and an astrologer?

3 A manned mission to Mars could happen soon. Describe what you think living on Mars would be like.

Language bank

astronomer
astronomy
astrophysicist
Uranus

Checkpoint

1 True or false?

Decide whether the following statements are true or false. Write down the true ones. Correct the false ones before you write them down.

a A day is the time it takes for the calendar to spin on its axis.

b A month is the time it takes for the Moon to orbit the Earth.

c A year is the time it takes for the Earth to orbit Neptune.

d We have different seasons because the Earth's axis is tilted.

2 Down under

Australia is in the southern hemisphere. When it is summer in the UK, it is winter in Australia.
Match up the beginnings and endings to make complete sentences.

Beginnings

When the southern hemisphere tilts towards the Sun,

It is winter in Australia when the southern hemisphere

It is summer in the UK when the northern hemisphere

In Australia, in the summer, the days

Endings

are longer and it is warmer.

the northern hemisphere tilts away from the Sun.

tilts away from the Sun.

tilts towards the Sun.

3 Eclipsed

Classify each of the following observations as a lunar eclipse or a solar eclipse. Write them in two different coloured lists. You could add a sketch of each eclipse showing the Earth, Moon and Sun.

Observations

A shadow passed in front of the Sun.

A shadow passed in front of the Moon.

The shadow was made by the Moon.

The shadow was made by the Earth.

The Moon was between the Sun and the Earth.

The Earth was between the Sun and the Moon.

4 Which planet?

Choose the correct description for each planet. Write a postcard from each one saying what it is like on the planet.

Planets

Venus

Jupiter

Earth

Saturn

Pluto

Descriptions

a year takes 365 days, atmosphere of nitrogen and oxygen

gravity is very very strong, it's cold

birthdays seem to come round quicker here, it's very hot

don't think I'll last long enough to have my first birthday, it's very cold

pretty rings, 24 moons

Glossary

Words in italic have their own glossary entry.

A

acid A substance with a *pH* lower than 7.

acid rain Rain that has become unnaturally acidic as a result of pollution.

adapted Able to survive in a certain set of environmental conditions.

adolescence The stage in human development between childhood and adulthood. It's a time of rapid physical and emotional development.

air resistance The *force* that acts against an object moving through air. Also known as drag.

alkali A substance with a *pH* higher than 7.

ammeter A device that measures electric *current*, usually in amps or milliamps.

amniotic fluid The liquid that surrounds a developing baby in the *uterus*.

antacid A substance used to treat indigestion by neutralising excess *acid* in the stomach.

anther The part of a plant that produces the *pollen*.

antibody A protein produced by the blood as a defence against harmful germs.

astronomy The study of planets, stars and space.

astrophysics The branch of physics that specialises in the study of space.

B

battery/cell A device for storing electricity as chemical energy.

boiling Changing a liquid into a gas by heating it.

C

cancer cells Abnormal *cells* that divide rapidly and uncontrollably, causing damage to organs.

carbon dioxide (CO2) A colourless, odourless gas found in the air. It is produced during *respiration* and *combustion* of fossil fuels, and by the reaction of *acid* with carbonates. It turns *limewater* cloudy.

carnivore A meat-eating animal, for example a lion or peregrine falcon.

carpel The female part of a plant, consisting of the *stigma*, style and *ovary*.

caustic substance A substance that burns or corrodes; the word is usually used to describe *alkalis*.

cell The smallest unit of a living *organism*.

cell membrane The thin outer layer that covers a *cell* and controls what enters and leaves the cell.

cell sap The liquid found in *cells*.

cell wall The rigid layer of a plant cell that covers the *cell membrane* and gives it shape.

cervix The narrow neck of the *uterus*, where it joins the *vagina*.

chlorophyll The green chemical in plants, used in *photosynthesis*.

chloroplast The part of a plant cell that contains the *chlorophyll*. *Photosynthesis* takes place inside the chloroplasts.

chromatography A way of separating substances in a *mixture*. The substances are moved across an absorbant surface by a *solvent*.

chromosome The part of a *cell* that contains genetic information. Chromosomes are responsible for passing on characteristics from parents to offspring.

circuit A wire loop containing electrical *components*, through which electricity can pass.

combustion Burning, where a substance like a fuel reacts with *oxygen*, giving out heat and light energy.

community All the *populations* of all the *species* living in the same area.

component Part of an electric *circuit*.

concentrated solution A *solution* containing a large amount of a *solute* in a certain volume of *solvent*.

conclusion A statement about what you have found out in an experiment or *investigation*.

condensation The process by which a gas changes into a liquid.

consumer An *organism* that eats plants and animals to survive.

contraception Avoiding pregnancy using natural or artificial methods.

corrosive substance A substance like an *acid* that might react with or eat away other materials.

coulomb (C) Unit of electrical charge.

current The flow of electrical charge or electricity in a *circuit*, measured in amps (A).

cytoplasm The material inside a living *cell*, excluding the *nucleus*.

D

data logger Electronic device used to take regular measurements of things like *pH* or temperature; it then allows the data to be dowloaded to a computer.

density How heavy something is for its size (mass ÷ volume).

diffusion The movement of *particles* from an area of high concentration to an area of low concentration.

dissolving The mixing of a *solute* with a *solvent* to make a *solution*.

distillation A separation technique that involves *evaporation*, then *condensation*.

DNA Deoxyribonucleic acid. The chemical that makes up *genes*.

dormancy Period of inactivity in the life of an *organism*, often over the winter.

E

eclipse The blocking of the Sun's light when the Moon is between the Earth and the Sun, or the blocking of the Moon's light when the Earth is between the Moon and the Sun.

effervesce To give off a gas.

embryo A young organism developing inside an egg, or inside its mother.

energy resource A material that can provide energy, for example coal, oil, and gas.

equation A way of representing a chemical reaction using symbols.

equator The imaginary line around the middle of the Earth.

evaporation The process by which a liquid changes into a gas.

F

fallopian tube The tube along which the egg cell travels from the *ovary* to the *uterus*. Also known as an oviduct.

fertilisation The joining of a male and a female sex cell to make a new living *organism*.

fetus An unborn human eight weeks or more after fertilisation.

fire triangle A diagram showing that heat, fuel, and a flame are needed for something to burn.

food chain Series of *organisms* that are dependent on one another for food. Each organism is eaten by the next in the chain.

food web All the food chains in a *community* joined together in a network.

force A push or a pull that one object exerts on another, measured in newtons (N).

forensic science The use of science and technology to solve crimes.

fossil fuel Fuel that comes from the remains of dead plants and animals, for example coal, oil, and natural gas.

freezing Changing from a liquid to a solid by cooling.

fuse A safety device used in electric *circuits*, which melts when the *current* gets too high, breaking the circuit.

G

galaxy A collection of stars and planets. Our galaxy is called the *Milky Way*.

genes Found on the *chromosomes* in the *nucleus*, they contain information about characteristics of an *organism*.

gestation The time between the fertilisation of the egg and birth, when the female animal carries her developing young inside her body. In humans, gestation is called pregnancy.

gravity The *force* that attracts two objects. Earth's gravity keeps everything on Earth from floating out into space.

H

habitat The place where a plant or animal lives.

herbivore An animal that eats only plants, for example a cow or a horse.

hibernation The way in which some animals survive the winter months, by going into a deep sleep.

hydrogen (H) A very low density but highly reactive gas produced by the reaction of *acid* with some metals. Makes a squeaky pop when a lighted splint is brought near a test tube of it.

I

indicator A substance that changes colour in the presence of an *acid* or an *alkali*.

inheritance Characteristics that an *organism* gets from its parents.

insoluble A substance that does not dissolve in a *solvent*.

invertebrate An *organism* that does not have a backbone.

investigation An experiment you do to prove or disprove a *theory*.

J

joule (J)/kilojoule (kJ) The unit for measuring energy (1kJ = 1000 J).

K

kilogram (kg) The unit for measuring mass.

L

life processes The seven things that all living things carry out to stay alive: movement, respiration, sensitivity, feeding, excretion, reproduction, and growth.

light year The distance that light travels in one year.

limewater A substance used to test for *carbon dioxide* gas. It turns cloudy in the presence of carbon dioxide.

litmus *Indicator* used to see if a substance is an *acid* or an *alkali*. It usually turns red in acid conditions and blue in alkaline conditions.

luminous object An object that is a source of light.

M

mammary gland A gland in the breasts of a female mammal that produces milk for the young.

melting Changing from a solid to a liquid by heating.

meniscus The surface or skin of a liquid.

menopause The time in a woman's life when she stops having periods.

menstrual cycle The cycle of regular monthly change that takes place in the female reproductive organs.

microscope An instrument used to view very small objects by forming a magnified image of them.

migration A regular journey made by some animals to reach breeding or feeding areas.

Milky Way The *galaxy* to which our *Solar System* belongs; the planets and stars we can see at night.

mixture Two or more substances mixed together. They are not chemically joined up, so can be separated.

N

natural gas Gas, mainly composed of methane, used in cooking and heating. It is found in many places, including under the North Sea.

neutral solution A *solution* with a *pH* of 7, which is neither acidic nor alkaline.

newton meter Device used to measure *force*.

nocturnal animal An animal that is active at night.

non-renewable resource An energy resource that will eventually 'run out', for example oil.

northern hemisphere The half of the Earth that is north of the *equator*.

nucleus The 'brain' of the *cell*, which controls what goes on in the cell.

O

organ Part of a living *organism* with a special function, for example the eye or heart.

organ system Many *organs* working together in an *organism*.

organism A living thing.

ovary The *organ* that produces female sex cells.

oviduct The tubes along which the egg cell travels from the *ovary* to the *uterus*. Also known as a fallopian tube

ovule The female sex cell in plants.

oxygen Colourless, odourless gas needed for *respiration* and *combustion* and produced during *photosynthesis*. Makes up 21% of air

P

parallel circuit An electric *circuit* with branches in it, so that the *current* divides between 'parallel' paths.

particle A minute piece of matter. Everything is made up of particles.

penis Male reproductive *organ*.

pH scale A scale of numbers from 0 to 14 used to measure acidity or alkalinity. *Acids* have a pH of less than 7 and *alkalis* have a pH of more than 7.

photosynthesis Process by which plants change *carbon dioxide* and water into food using sunlight and *chlorophyll*.

placenta The *organ* in female mammals where exchange of nutrients and waste between the mother and the growing *fetus* in the *uterus* happens.

pollen The part of a flower that contains the male sex cells.

pollen tube The tube that develops when *pollen* lands on the *stigma* of a plant so the pollen can reach the eggs in the *ovary*.

population The number of members of one particular *species* in a *habitat*.

precipitate The solid produced in some chemical reactions, which often falls to the bottom of the test tube.

predator An *organism* that hunts prey for food.

pregnancy The time when a female animal has a developing *fetus* in her *uterus*.

pressure The amount of *force* with which a liquid or gas pushes on a surface. Increases with depth in a liquid.

prey An *organism* that is hunted by a *predator*.

producer Green plant, which produces its own food, found at the start of a *food chain* or *web*.

pure substance A single substance that is not a *mixture*.

R

reflection Light or sound bouncing back off an object.

renewable energy An energy resource that once used can be replaced naturally, and will not 'run out', for example wind power.

resistance A measure of how hard it is to push an electric *current* through a substance.

respiration The process by which living things release energy from their food using *oxygen*.

S

salt The substance that forms when an *acid* reacts with an *alkali*.

satellite A small object in orbit around a larger one; moons are natural satellites.

series circuit An electric *circuit* with no branches in it.

short circuit A fault in an electric *circuit* that allows the *current* to take a short cut, bypassing part of the circuit.

Solar System The Sun and the family of planets and other objects that orbit around it.

solubility The amount of a substance (*solute*) that will dissolve in a certain amount of liquid (*solvent*). Usually stated at a certain temperature.

solute The substance that dissolves in a *solvent*, forming a *solution*.

solution The *mixture* formed when a *solute* dissolves in a *solvent*.

solvent The liquid in which a *solute* dissolves to form a *solution*.

specialised cells *Cells* that are well suited to a certain job.

species A group of similar *organisms* that can breed together to produce fertile offspring.

speed A measure of how fast something is travelling, in metres per second.

sperm The male sex *cell* in animals, which joins with the female sex cell to produce offspring.

stamen The male parts of a flower.

state of matter The three forms in which matter can exist – solid, liquid or gas.

stigma Top part of the female reproductive *organ* in a flowering plant, which receives the pollen.

theory A statement that can be proved or disproved by an experiment or *investigation*.

tissue A group of similar *cells* that do a job together.

tumour A ball of abnormal *cells* that invades and damages *organs*.

umbilical cord The tube that joins the *fetus* to the *placenta*.

unicellular organism An *organism* that is made of only one *cell*.

universal indicator A mixture of *indicators* that gives a certain colour at a certain *pH*.

universe Everything that exists, including the Earth, its creatures, and the heavenly bodies.

upthrust A *force* exerted by water.

uterus The *organ* in the female body where a *fetus* develops. Also known as the womb.

vacuole A fluid-filled bag or sac found in the *cytoplasm* of living *cells*.

vacuum Complete emptiness; the total absence of air or any other material.

vagina The part of the female reproductive system that receives the penis, and connects the *uterus* to the outside.

variation Differences between members of the same *species*.

vertebrate An *organism* that has a backbone (spine), for example a bird or a mammal.

virus A microscopic *organism* that reproduces by infecting a living *cell*. Colds and chicken-pox are caused by viruses.

voltage A measure of the strength or push an electrical supply gives a *circuit*.

weight The *force* with which a mass is pulled down to Earth as a result of *gravity*.

womb *see* uterus

Z

zygote The *cell* that forms after a *sperm* fertilises an egg.

Index

Acknowledgements

t= top, l = left, r = right, c = centre, b = bottom.
SPL = Science Photo Library
OSF = Oxford Scientific Films
NHPA = Natural History Photo Library
BBC NHU = BBC Natural History Unit
BCTNW = Bruce Coleman The Natural World

Cover photo: Photodisc and Digitalvision

p7 Photodisc; p8 Chase Swift/Corbis; p9t Manfred Kage/SPL, 9c David Becker/SPL, 9b Biology Media/SPL; 10l SPL, 10c D. Phillips/SPL, 10r OSF; p11t Colin Cuthbert/SPL, 11c Moredun Animal Health/ SPL, 11r Dr. P. Marazzi/SPL; p12 A&H Frieder Michler/SPL; p14l SPL, 14c Andrew Syred/SPL, 14r Andrew Syred/SPL; p15 Paddy Gannon; p17 Alfred Pasieka/ SPL; p19 Photodisc; p20t D. Phillips/SPL. 20l Kim Taylor/ BCTNW, 20r Owen Newman/OSF; p22cr Mantis Wildlife Films/ OSF, 22 bl Petit Format/Nestle/SPL, 22bc Petit Format/ Nestle/ SPL, 22br Dr Derek Bromhall/OSF; p23 Paddy Gannon; p24 Keith/Custom medical stock/SPL; 25t Neil Bromhall/OSF, 25l Stephen J. Krasemann/SPL, 25r Wayne Bilenduke/Getty Images; p28c James King-Holmes/SPL, 28b CNRI/SPL; p29c Oxford University Press, 29l Paddy Gannon; p31 Corel; p32l Phil Redmond/Brookside, 32r David Hosking/ SPL; p33tl B & C Alexander, 33tr Robert Weight/Ecoscene, 33cl Sami Sarkis/ Alamy, 33cr Douglas P. Wilson/Corbis; p34 background & cl Ron Watts/Corbis, 34cr Peter Johnson/Corbis, 34bl Bob Glover/ BCTNW, 34bcl Kim Taylor/BCTNW, 34bcr Ingo Arndt/BBC NHU, 34br OSF; p35t Daniel Cox/OSF, 35c OSF, 35cr (both) Paddy Gannon; p36 all Griffin & George/ www.griffinandgeorge.co.uk except: 36tr H. Rogers/Trip, 36tc Paddy Gannon, 36c Paddy Gannon, 36cr Paddy Gannon, 36bl Nigel Cattlin/Holt Studios; p37 Dr. Eckart Pott/NHPA; p38cl Norbert Wu/NHPA, 38c Christophe Ratier/ NHPA, 38cr James Carmichael JR/NHPA, 38bl Mark Hamblin/ OSF, 38bc Richard Anthony/Holt Studios, 38br BCTNW; p39tr Norbert Wu/NHPA, 39cl Jane Burton/ BCTNW; p41 Roger Tidman/NHPA; p43 Corel; p44t Jeanne White/SPL, 44cl OSF, 44c Max Gibbs/OSF; p46bl Oxford University Press, 46br Durand Patrick/Corbis Sygma; p47l Nigel Cattlin/Holt Studios, 47r Nigel Cattlin/Holt Studios; p52 SPL; p55 Stockbyte; p56t Debra Weatherley, 56b Paddy Gannon, Oxford University Press; p57t Paddy Gannon, 57cl Biofoto Associates/SPL, 57cr Corel; p58l Paddy Gannon, 58r Paddy Gannon; p59 Erik de Castro/Reuters/ Popperfoto; p60tc Paddy Gannon, 60tr Paddy Gannon, 60c Paddy Gannon, 60b Paddy Gannon; p61 Eye of Science/SPL; p62cl Paddy Gannon, 62c David Nunuk/SPL, 62b Ted Spiegel/Corbis; p63 Peter Gould; p65 Corel; p66l Alex Bartel/SPL, 66c Peter Gould; p68 Paddy Gannon; p69 Paddy Gannon (all); p70l Paddy Gannon, 70r Charles D. Winters/SPL; p72tl Martin Bond/SPL, 72tr Peter Gould, 72cl Erich Schrempp/SPL, 72cr Paddy Gannon, 72bl

Paddy Gannon, 72br Dorling Kindersley; p75 Photodisc; p76l Adam Jones/SPL, 76c Martin Bond/SPL, 76r John Sanford/SPL; p78 Joan Hickson/Moviestore Collection; p82 Martyn F. Chillmaid/SPL; p84t Peter Gould, 84b Tek Image/ SPL; p85c Peter Gould, 85r Corbis; p89 Photodisc; p90 Salt Union Ltd; 91 Mark Edwards/Still Pictures; p92 Pascal Goetgheluck/SPL; p93tr Oleg Popov/Reuters/Popperfoto, 93cl Geoff Tompkinson/ SPL, 93br Photodisk; p94 Peter Gould; p96 Corel; p97 David Parker/SPL; p99 Photodisc; p100tl Kaj R. Svensson/SPL. 100tc Sami Sarkis/Alamy.com. 100tr Peter Gould; p102t Paddy Gannon, 102l Cordelia Molloy/SPL, 102cl Sami Sarkis/ Alamy.com, 102cr Paddy Gannon, 102r Dr. Jeremy Burgess/SPL, 102bl The Flight Collection; p104t Alex Bartel/ SPL, 104l Alex Bartel/SPL, 104cl Paddy Gannon, 104cr Martin Bond/SPL, Paddy Gannon; p105tl Martin Bond/ SPL, 105tr Martin Bond/ SPL, 105cl Simon Fraser/SPL, 105cr Martin Bond/SPL; p106 Paddy Gannon; p107l Fiat Ecobasic/ FIAT, 107r Paddy Gannon; p111 Digitalvision; p117 David Buffington/Getty Images; p118 Martyn F. Chillmaid/SPL; p119t Dr. Jeremy Burgess/SPL, 119b Paddy Gannon; p120 Paddy Gannon; p121 Corbis; p122 Paddy Gannon; p123 Adam Hart-Davis/SPL; p125 Corel; p128 Sutton Motorsport; p130t The Car Photo Library, 130b Photodisc/Getty Images/Cadmium; p131 The Car Photo Library; p132 Richard T. Nowitz/Corbis; p133t Corel, 133b Photodisc; p134 Brian Erler/TCL/Getty Images; p137 Photodisc; p138 Arnulf Husmo/Getty Images; p141l, 141r StockTrek/Photodisc; p142tl US Geological Survey/SPL, 142tc, 142tr StockTrek/ Photodisc, 142cl StockTrek/Photodisc, 142c StockTrek/ Photodisc, 142cr NASA, 142bl NASA, 142bc NASA, 142br NASA/SPL; p144tl StockTrek/Photodisc, 144tc NASA/SPL, 144tr Detlev Van Ravenswaay/SPL, 144bl Eckhard Slawik/SPL; p145t David Nunuk/SPL, 145c Space telescope Science Institute/SPL, 145b NASA; p146t NASA, 146c SPL, 146bl SPL, 146br David Parker/SPL; p147t NASA, 147b David Ducros/SPL

Photo research by Debra Weatherley.
Technical illustrations are by Oxford Designers & Illustrators.
Cartoons are by John Hallet.

We are grateful to the following for permission to reproduce copyright material in this book.
Google Inc for Google™ UK homepage screen shot. Google™ is a trademark of Google Inc.
HarperCollins Publisher Ltd for extract from *Collins Gem Guide: Birds* by Martin Woodcock and Richard Perry, copyright © 1980 Martin Woodcock and Richard Perry
The Random House Group Ltd for 'Caterpillar' by Norman MacCaig from *Collected Poems of Norman MacCaig* (Chatto and Windus, 1987).